ERROL FLYNN

ERROL FLYNN

A Pyramid Illustrated History of the Movies

by
GEORGE MORRIS

General Editor: **TED SENNETT**

PUBLICATIONS
New York

For my grandmother Bessie

ERROL FLYNN
A PYRAMID ILLUSTRATED HISTORY OF THE MOVIES

Pyramid edition published July 1975

ISBN 0-515-03739-7

Library of Congress Catalog Card Number: 75-4184

Printed in the United States of America

Pyramid Books are published by Pyramid Communications, Inc. Its trademarks, consisting of the word "Pyramid" and the portrayal of a pyramid, are registered in the United States Patent Office.

Pyramid Communications, Inc., 919 Third Avenue, New York, N.Y. 10022

(graphic design by anthony basile)

ACKNOWLEDGMENTS

I wish to express my profound thanks for the help and encouragement the following people gave me in the preparation of this book:
Arlene Balkansky, Susan Dalton, Steve Masar, and George Talbot of the Wisconsin Center for Theatre Research, Madison, Wisconsin; Joseph Seechack in the film library of WNEW-TV, Channel 5, New York; Jim Stark; Charles Silver; Howard Mandelbaum and Roger McNiven, whose discussions with me on *The Sea Hawk* and *Gentleman Jim* have proven invaluable; William Dolive; Ted Sennett, my editor; Andrew Sarris, without whom none of this would have been possible; and last, but far from least, my parents.

Photographs: Jerry Vermilye, The Memory Shop, Movie Star News, Gene Andrewski, and the studios that produced the films of Errol Flynn.

CONTENTS

> *"I want to be taken seriously . . . I allow myself to be understood abroad as a colorful fragment in a drab world."* —Errol Flynn

INTRODUCTION: KING OF THE SWASHBUCKLERS

Errol Flynn was a true original. Douglas Fairbanks may have been the prototype for the swashbuckling roles Flynn inherited, but it is doubtful that Fairbanks could have equaled the diversity and range Flynn brought to such roles as George Custer, James Corbett, and Mike McComb. Flynn played the devil-may-care adventurer better than anyone else, but his most interesting performances revealed the dark underside of this image. In many of his roles, Flynn was not afraid to drop the mask of the dashing rogue, allowing his fans a glimpse of a vulnerability and helplessness akin to that of a small boy lost in a man's world.

The comparisons with Fairbanks are inevitable, but the differences in their respective personae are illuminating. Fairbanks was a prototype formed during the halcyon days of the silent cinema. Stars of his era seemed to be from another planet, so remote were their public images from the everyday world of most viewers. When sound revolutionized the industry, however, the distance between audiences and stars narrowed, resulting in a demand for more recognizable, lifelike idols. Thirties moviegoers wanted Joan Blondell instead of Theda Bara, James Cagney over John Gilbert, and Errol Flynn rather than Douglas Fairbanks.

Most of the time, Flynn *was* larger than life; he indisputably had that intangible element known as "star quality." But he was also human. He descended from the Mount Olympus of movie stardom often enough to be acceptable to changing mores and audience standards.

Flynn was also fortunate in his timing. People went to the movies during the Depression to forget the financial turmoil rippling through the nation. They wanted escape and adventure, and in 1935, when an incredibly attractive young man swung across the screen on the rigging of a pirate vessel for the first time, he connected with this audience. Flynn's dash and vigor inspired the young, excited the women, and rejuvenated the men. Flynn's low-key acting style made it easy for audiences to identify with him, so that the more idealistic males in the audience strutted out of movie houses, convinced that any derring-do Flynn could do, they could at least *dream* about doing better.

10

Flynn's immense popularity with his female audience cannot be underestimated. Flynn's appeal to women was a curious mixture of mock chivalry and sexual aggression. Extending a tradition begun by Cagney's grapefruit uppercut to Mae Clarke in 1931, there is an undercurrent of hostility and indifference in Flynn's attitude toward women running throughout his films. However, his undeniable charm and impudence mesmerized the ladies, serving as vital restraints in preventing this aggressive attitude from lapsing into overt misogyny. His ardent wooing of Olivia de Havilland often seems tongue-in-cheek, and his most passionate vows of love are always mitigated by the vanity and ego he exudes in every scene. Richard Schickel has described Flynn's onscreen technique as "using the act of love as an act of aggression," a comparison that reflected Flynn's offscreen reputation as well.

Flynn's hell-raising screen image coincided with a private life that was punctuated with peccadilloes and various scandals, all of which were juicily detailed in fan magazines and newspapers. A scandalous paternity suit brought against him in the early forties merely increased his box-office power. These offscreen escapades reinforced his fans' preconceptions and aroused the curiosity of others.

The rebel aspect was always an important part of Flynn's screen persona in any case. He played a rebel of one kind or another in almost all of his best films. There is a strong anti-authoritarian impulse hovering beneath the surface of his most interesting characterizations—an impulse that usually emerges at a crucial moment in the narrative. He rebels against the tyranny of James II in *Captain Blood*, forges orders to make the *Charge of the Light Brigade*, is an intractable recalcitrant in *The Sisters*, and burns a Union payroll in *Silver River*. Numerous Flynn vehicles find him disobeying orders from those higher in authority. Who is Robin Hood anyway, but one of the most defiant, colorful anti-authoritarian folklore figures?

Flynn's personal life, before stardom as well as during it, provided a rich source of experiences for the actor to utilize in his roles. Like a great many stars, the distinction between Flynn's private and public image was often blurred. The adventurer and the lover worked both sides of the screen. The reality often reflected the illusion, and the illusion reinforced the reality in the minds of a most susceptible and willing public.

Flynn's early life reads like an exaggerated scenario for one of his adventure films. Even as a child, Flynn was no stranger to rebellion. He acquired an early and lasting distaste for the staid, conservative life. Born on June 20, 1909, in Hobart, Tasmania, a seaport of the British Commonwealth, he was strongly influenced by the ocean throughout most of his life. His mother was the daughter of a sea captain, and his father was a renowned marine biologist. Time and again, Flynn would forsake his career for a sporadic return to the sea in one of the various schooners he was to own. The ocean, and its implicit promise of endless freedom and adventure, paradoxically became a symbol of stability and certainty in Flynn's somewhat precarious existence.

Flynn never got along very well with his mother, but he idolized his father. Professor Theodore Thomson Flynn, a distinguished faculty member of the University of Tasmania, was later appointed the Royal Commissioner of Tasmanian Fisheries, and in 1931, assumed a post at Queen's University in Belfast, as a professor of biology, a commission that necessitated a move to Northern Ireland.

Flynn was, to put it mildly, a problem child. The strain to live up to the expectations and achievements of the father he so revered,

THE EARLY YEARS: STARDOM WITH CAPTAIN BLOOD

combined with the lack of maternal rapport, created very real psychological and emotional problems during his adolescence. An excellent sportsman (he particularly excelled at boxing and swimming), he was nevertheless expelled from many good schools. He found it difficult to maintain interest in any one subject and never followed a job through to its conclusion.

Flynn did a bit of everything in his early youth. He clerked for a shipping company in Australia, served as a cadet in the New Guinea government service, oversaw a copra plantation, ran a small charter schooner up and down the Australian coast, mined gold, and, when all else failed, rather unscrupulously recruited native labor for the gold mines.

The turning point in Flynn's life occurred in 1930. The enterprising young soldier-of-fortune invested in a fifty-year-old schooner, which he christened the *Sirocco*, and began chartering voyages along the Great Barrier Reef. One of his clients was Dr. Herman F. Erben, a specialist in tropical diseases and an amateur filmmaker. Dr. Erben hired Flynn to sail him up the Sepik River in New Guinea to photograph a group

14

As a young contract player at Warners

IN THE WAKE OF THE BOUNTY (1933). As Fletcher Christian

of primitive headhunters. During the course of the two-month expedition, Dr. Erben just happened to shoot a few pictures of Flynn on deck.

That old maxim of being in the right place at the right time certainly applies to Flynn's discovery, for those idly snapped photos of Flynn cavorting with crocodiles fell into the hands, two years later, of Charles Chauvel, an Australian film producer and director. Chauvel immediately contacted Flynn, and offered him the role of Fletcher Christian in *In the Wake of the Bounty*. Flynn accepted.

The seventy-minute film was shot in three weeks, and sported a vastly inexperienced Flynn in a blond wig, looking terribly ill-at-ease as Mayne Lynton, playing Captain Bligh, chewed the somewhat artificial scenery. Flynn had never acted at all, and his lack of experience is painfully evident.

The film itself is a curiosity piece, a hodgepodge of documentary footage shot on Pitcairn Island, amateurish acting, and singularly static dramatic scenes. All in all, it was an inauspicious debut for the young Flynn.

When MGM decided to produce its own version of the tale as *Mutiny on the Bounty*, the studio bought the rights to the Australian feature, incorporating much of the documentary footage into promo-

tional shorts, heralding their own much more lavish production. *In the Wake of the Bounty* was never released theatrically in the United States.

In his autobiography, Flynn describes with some amusement the experience of making a personal appearance at the theater in Sydney on the evening of the film's premiere:

"The manager made an announcement before the picture was flashed on the screen. He said that Errol Flynn, who would appear as Fletcher Christian in the picture, was here in person. I was decked out in a bizarre out-of-date British uniform. There were only two actors' wigs in Sydney they could find and they stuck one of them on me. It was parted in the middle and it came down in a pigtail in the back, blonde, tied with a bow . . . and clapped over my ears so that I reminded myself vividly of an elderly keeper of a whorehouse in King William Street, a little place of some integrity which I was prone to frequent." *

Flynn's feature film debut didn't exactly set the Australian film industry on fire, and shortly thereafter, he found himself broke and drifting once again from job to job. He managed a tobacco plantation

*Errol Flynn, *My Wicked, Wicked Ways* (New York: G.P. Putnam's Sons, 1959), p. 100.

for a while at Laloki, and also began writing columns on diverse aspects of New Guinea life for the *Sydney Bulletin*.

Increasingly restless with his peripatetic existence Down Under, and with his appetite whetted by his one brush with acting, Flynn connived his way to England to pursue an acting career. Arriving in London in the spring of 1933, he found breaking into the film studios there a bit more difficult than he had expected. He *did* manage, however, to land a job acting with the Northampton Repertory Company. The actor remained with this troupe in the English Midlands well over a year, accompanying it to London for various limited engagements. During one of these sojourns to the West End, Flynn finagled a meeting with Irving Asher, the managing director of the Warner Bros.-First National studios in Teddington.

Flynn's brash self-assertion and roguish good looks prompted Asher to sign him to a contract—without even a screen test. He was thrust immediately into the lead in *Murder at Monte Carlo*, one of the many quota quickies enabling the British film industry to remain afloat during the Depression.

At the tennis matches with friend and wife Lili Damita

THE CASE OF THE CURIOUS BRIDE (1935). With Margaret Lindsay

Released in 1935, *Murder at Monte Carlo* revealed a terribly self-conscious Flynn as a newspaper reporter on an assignment in the gambling capital to expose a crooked roulette system. Most of the cast took back seats to Paul Graetz's overwrought portrayal of the inventor of the roulette system. (*Film Weekly* commented at the time that "the whole cast suffers from comparison with Paul Graetz's fine performance.")

The critics may not have been overly impressed with Flynn's performance, but Irving Asher certainly was. He urged Jack Warner to send for Flynn upon completion of the film, and in 1935, the actor sailed for America, a six-month contract with the studio at $150 per week under his belt.

Flynn met the actress, Lili Damita, on the ship, and the two were married in June of the same year. Divorced seven years later in 1942, their tempestuous marriage produced one son, Sean, who was lost at sea on a sailing expedition in the late sixties.

Now that Jack Warner had Flynn under contract at his studio, the problem arose as to the most appropriate showcase for the young actor's unproven thespic abilities. For a few months, Flynn languished around the studio as merely another hopeful contract player. A part in Max Reinhardt's *A Midsummer Night's Dream* fell through. When he finally landed his first assignment in Hollywood, it was the singularly unpromising role of a corpse in a Perry Mason B-movie, *The Case of the Curious Bride*. In addition to his brief stint as a corpse, Flynn also had a sixty-second scene with no dialogue, during which Margaret Lindsay knocked him unconscious with a poker.

The film itself is a snappy little murder mystery full of humor and inventiveness, unpretentiously directed by Michael Curtiz, the first of twelve films he was to direct with Flynn.

Flynn's second film at Warner Bros. in 1935 was another programmer, although much less expert than the Curtiz movie. *Don't Bet On Blondes* starred Warren William (Perry Mason in the earlier film) as a gambler who insures Guy Kibbee against his wealthy daughter's cutting off his income. Predictably, romantic complications develop between William and the daughter (Claire Dodd). Under

DON'T BET ON BLONDES (1935). As a society playboy with dubious friends

CAPTAIN BLOOD (1935). As Dr. Peter Blood

Robert Florey's uninspired direction, Flynn was cast as a society playboy who vies with William for Miss Dodd's hand. Flynn has two short scenes, totaling approximately five minutes of screen time.

The release of *Treasure Island* and *The Count of Monte Cristo* in 1934, and *Mutiny on the Bounty* in 1935, initiated an adventure film cycle in Hollywood. The success of a particular kind of film has always spawned countless efforts to imitate and duplicate, and this trend was no exception. Sir Walter Scott, Robert Louis Stevenson, Alexandre Dumas, and Rafael Sabatini were dusted off by the moguls and mined for their potential box-office values.

Warner Bros. jumped on the bandwagon with Sabatini's *Captain Blood,* which had previously been filmed in 1924 with J. Warren Kerrigan. Elaborate plans were made for a remake with Robert Donat as Peter Blood, the physician who is forced to become a buccaneer, and Jean Muir as the highborn lady of Port Royal who wins his heart.

A breakdown in contractual negotiations between the studio and Donat found Warners needing a leading man fast. Jack Warner decided to have director Michael Curtiz test the handsome young Tasmanian who had been hanging around the studio for several months. A test was filmed with Olivia de Havilland, and both rela-

tive newcomers won the leading roles. Once again, Flynn had just happened to be in the right place at the right time, just as he had a few years previously on that fortuitous voyage up the Sepik River when Dr. Erben had photographed him at the helm of the *Sirocco.*

Flynn more than confirmed the faith that Warner and Curtiz had placed in him. Although nearly two weeks' footage was shelved and re-shot because the actor gained more confidence as filming progressed, the final result firmly established Errol Flynn as the swashbuckler *par excellence.* All of the elements of the Flynn persona are present in his portrayal of Peter Blood—the fervor, the gallantry, the open sincerity, the impudent charm, the rebelliousness, and the invigorating energy that were to characterize his best performances for years to come.

The film itself is a lusty yarn calculated to inspire the young and regale the old with its picaresque locales, exciting action set pieces, and sweeping romance. Flynn plays a former adventurer (Irish, of course), turned physician during the perfidious reign of King James II. Condemned for high treason when he ministers to a wounded rebel, he is exiled to Port Royal, an English colony in the Caribbean, to be sold into slavery.

On the island, the dashing Blood

CAPTAIN BLOOD (1935). With Colin Kenny and Guy Kibbee

is bought for ten pounds by the niece of a plantation owner (Olivia de Havilland). When the governor of the island discovers Blood is a doctor, he sends for him to treat his gout. His contact with the governor delights his owner, who is attracted to him, and enrages her uncle (Lionel Atwill), a typical Curtiz sadist who has a penchant for using a branding iron on slaves who attempt to escape.

When pirates working under King Philip of Spain loot and pillage the English colony, Blood escapes with a contingent of slaves, rallies the Spanish pirates' boat, and assumes a life of piracy on the Caribbean. When King William and Queen Mary ascend the throne, they pardon Blood and appoint him as the new governor of Port Royal. The final scene reunites Flynn with de Havilland as he assumes his new post.

Captain Blood was a first for Flynn in many respects. It was his first starring role under Curtiz, his first real swashbuckler (a genre in which he was to have no serious

CAPTAIN BLOOD (1935). With Olivia de Havilland

challengers), his first film of seven to be scored by the prolific Erich Wolfgang Korngold, and his first to co-star de Havilland. The two proved to be such a popular team that they were to make eight more films together.

The foundation for the thrust-and-parry nature of their screen relationship is laid in *Captain Blood*. When de Havilland saucily admonishes Flynn for talking treason by speaking against her uncle, the rogue rejoins: "I hope I'm not being obscure." Their courting patterns are also firmly established in this film. When Flynn overreaches his familiarity by kissing her, de Havilland slaps him. Flynn's first impulse is to strike her back. He lurches forward and then smiles impishly. His devil-may-care chivalry and her haughty flirtatiousness set the tone for one of the most felicitous screen teams of the late thirties and early forties.

Captain Blood also introduces the prototypical duel which was to climax every Flynn swashbuckler. Basil Rathbone's Captain Levasseur forms an uneasy alliance with Blood on Tortuga, the colorful haven of safety for all pirates. When Rathbone threatens de Havilland's life, Flynn challenges him to a duel on the rocky seashore, a brief but exciting precursor to the lengthier, more elaborate clashes of swords that will follow in *The Adventures of Robin Hood* and *The Sea Hawk*.

There is a moment in *Captain Blood*, peculiar to movies, in which the configuration of a myth emerges on the screen. When Flynn and his fellow slaves from Port Royal take over the Spanish pirate ship, the unfurling of the sails is accompanied by the men's singing lustily as the anchor of the vessel is lifted. Flynn strides boldly around the deck, giving the necessary orders, and in an extraordinary series of close-ups, Curtiz presents us with the emergence of a star. It is an exhilarating sequence, its effect not easily explained by mere words, intangible yet concrete; once having seen it, one can easily understand why *Captain Blood* turned Errol Flynn into a star virtually overnight.

With Flynn's swashbuckler image firmly entrenched in the public eye upon the release of *Captain Blood*, Warner Bros. lost no time in setting their publicity wheels in motion in order to familiarize every segment of the filmgoing audience with their new star. Stories were circulated in the fan magazines about Flynn's early life in Australia and his prowess with the ladies. He appeared in a Technicolor two-reel featurette early in 1936, *Pirate Party On Catalina Isle,* released by MGM, and also featuring such luminaries as his wife, Lili Damita, Marion Davies, Cary Grant, Virginia Bruce, Chester Morris, Lee Tracy, and John Gilbert.

Flynn apparently loved all the publicity he began to receive. His amorous escapades kept the gossip columnists happy and the fans interested. His reputation as a great adventurer and an ardent lover was being subtly consolidated by the high-powered Hollywood publicity machinery. People were curious about every aspect of the handsome young star's life, from his recurrent bouts with malaria and tuberculosis to his 4-F draft rating because of an "athletic heart."

Meanwhile, Warners lost no time in thrusting Flynn into another epic adventure story, *The Charge of the Light Brigade,* again co-starring Olivia de Havilland, and again directed by Michael Curtiz. *Charge*

ROBIN HOOD AND OTHER HEROES

has its fair share of thrills, but the characters are not as well developed as those in *Captain Blood.* Set on the Crimean frontier in the mid-nineteenth century, the film casts Flynn as a major of the British 27th Lancers, de Havilland as his somewhat neglected fiancée, and Patric Knowles as his brother, the object of de Havilland's true affections. The most unusual aspect of this triangle—de Havilland's continuing preference for Knowles over Flynn, the star of the film—is peremptorily treated by Curtiz, and the potential variations in playing against an audience's expectations are never explored. As in most of his adventure films, Curtiz seems more interested in the broad strokes of the action sequences than he is in nuance of behavior or depth of characterization.

If the characters in *Charge of the Light Brigade* emerge as little more than one-dimensional stereotypes, the action sequences certainly do not disappoint. Curtiz magnificently handles the big set pieces—a leopard hunt to the ominous beating of drums; Surat Khan's attack on Chukoti, a montage of exploding cannon, screaming women and

THE CHARGE OF THE LIGHT BRIGADE (1936). With Olivia de Havilland

THE CHARGE OF THE LIGHT BRIGADE (1936). With Olivia de Havilland

children, and ladders being thrown up against the white walls of the fort, the dark figures of fighting men silhouetted against the sky; and, of course, the charge itself—one of the most superbly staged action sequences in the cinema. The pulsating rhythms of Max Steiner's musical score beautifully parallel the action rhythms of this sequence, beginning with the stately march of the horses and accelerating into the frenzied charge itself. Curtiz alternates sweeping long shots and exhilarating parallel tracks with closeups of wounded lancers, falling horses, and individual hand-to-hand combat.

Flynn swaggers through his role with great aplomb, exuding much more confidence than he had in *Captain Blood*, even though the role itself is not as interesting. The film would have had greater impact if Curtiz had followed through the darker implications of his character. Flynn takes de Havilland's love for granted in the film; he seems totally oblivious of her needs and desires. His reaction to the knowledge that she loves his brother, is that of a "little man." A dark, brooding look comes over his features as he receives the news, but instead of using these disturbing tendencies in Flynn's performance as a springboard to a more complex revelation of character, Curtiz is content to allow Flynn to sulk and pout

throughout the rest of the film.

Flynn is absolved in the end when he forces Knowles to stay behind from the suicidal charge for de Havilland's sake, an ultimate act of sacrifice that is supposed to mitigate Flynn's previous childish behavior. The rebel element in the actor's persona surfaces near the end of the film when he forges the orders that allow the 27th Lancers to avenge themselves against Khan for the massacre of their garrison at Chukoti.

The year 1937 brought the publication of Flynn's first novel, *Beam Ends,* in which the hero, based loosely on the author, stands trial for murder of a native marauder in the New Guinea jungle. The book did little for Flynn's literary reputation, even though the actor was to claim all his life that he loved writing more than acting, and, in fact, felt far more creative wielding a pen than a sword.

Early that year, Flynn traveled to Spain to get a glimpse of the civil conflict dividing the country. Rumors floated back to the United States that he had been killed in the fighting there, but Warner Bros. quickly proved the reports to be exaggerated.

Flynn also made four movies in 1937. The most notable of these was Frank Borzage's touching filmization of Lloyd C. Douglas' *Green Light.* Flynn portrayed a successful

THE CHARGE OF THE LIGHT BRIGADE (1936). Leading the charge

young doctor who assumes the blame for the failure of an operation that results in the death of a patient. Refusing to break the confidence of the Hippocratic Oath, Flynn's respect for professional ethics leads him first to whiskey and then to heroics, as he allows a wood tick to burrow into his hide in order to discover a vaccine against spotted fever.

Borzage transforms Douglas' sophomoric dialectic between the present and eternity into an awesome affirmation of faith, more mystical than religious and more cosmic than Christian. Flynn gives a muted performance, in marked contrast to the dashing bravura he communicates in his adventure films.

In his second effort of 1937, *The Prince and the Pauper*, Flynn does not even appear until midway through the film. William Keighley's lively if overlong version of Mark Twain's novel is primarily a vehicle for the Mauch Twins, Billy and Bobby, who respectively portray the pauper taken for Prince Edward, and Prince Edward mistaken for Tom Canty, the pauper of Offal Court.

Flynn comes into the film as a soldier-of-fortune at an opportune moment, rescuing the disguised prince from a band of marauding ruffians and befriending him with a leg of mutton and a place to sleep. The actor still has time to flirt with a serving wench in the midst of his adventures, however, and the insolence that was rapidly becoming an important part of his image is demonstrated when he sits at the foot of the throne during his young friend's coronation. *The Prince and the Pauper* was the first film Flynn made with his good friend, Alan Hale. The two were to make twelve films together during the years they were both under contract to Warner Bros..

Another Dawn found Flynn back in the desert, battling between moral responsibility and ardent passion as he falls in love with the wife (Kay Francis) of his commanding officer (Ian Hunter). Director William Dieterle lacks the conviction necessary to pull off this project, and the romance comes out rather turgid, stymied at every turn by the heavy-handed philosophizing in which each of the characters indulges.

Flynn's final film of the year, *The Perfect Specimen*, is an interesting attempt to capitalize humorously on the actor's developing screen personality. Based on a story by Samuel Hopkins Adams, *The Perfect Specimen* centers on Flynn as a wealthy heir who has been groomed by his grandmother (May Robson, in a delicious performance) to be mentally, morally, and physically superior. Incredibly sheltered and ingenuous when it comes to the

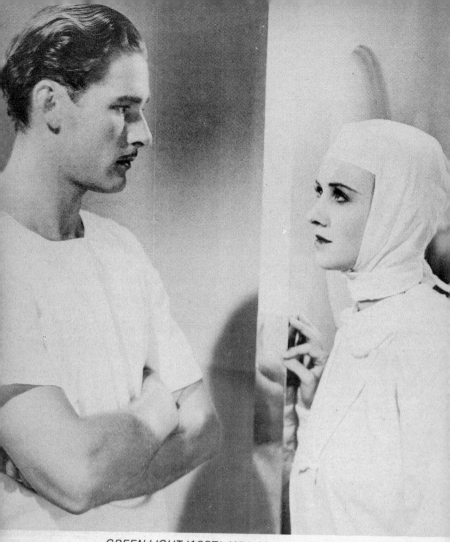

GREEN LIGHT (1937). With Margaret Lindsay

ways of the world, Flynn is convinced by wisecracking reporter Joan Blondell to desert his private sanctuary and see a bit of the real world, with her as his personal guide.

It all sounds much more delightful than it plays. Director Michael Curtiz paces the comedy very sluggishly; the picaresque incidents that punctuate Blondell and Flynn's journeys are neither well developed

THE PRINCE AND THE PAUPER (1937). With Bobby Mauch

nor particularly amusing. Also, Flynn and his co-star evince little rapport toward one another. Casting Flynn in a part that mocks and exaggerates the very qualities that made him a star was a marvelous idea, but the satire is too imprecise and the narrative too diffuse for any real comic effect.

Every great screen actor who achieves a mythic immortality has at least one role with which his name is

ANOTHER DAWN (1937). With Kay Francis, Ian Hunter, and Frieda Inescort

synonymous. In 1938 Errol Flynn assayed the part that was to propel him beyond mere stardom to a plateau reserved for the very few. *The Adventures of Robin Hood* assures Flynn a permanent niche in the iconography of the cinema. It is the role for which he will be most remembered, and it is easily his most engaging, assured performance under director Michael Curtiz. *Robin Hood* itself is a film by which other adventure films are measured. In the thirty-seven years since its release, it has lost none of its power to sweep the viewer up in its timeless story, bold adventure,

and romantic gusto. Watching it today, one experiences startling intimations of the primitive energy that drew most people to the movies in the first place.

James Cagney was originally slated to star as Sir Robin of Locksley, but the fortuitous convergence of one of Cagney's contractual disputes and the release of *Captain Blood*, convinced Warners to develop the property for Flynn instead. The film, culled from the various ballads and tales surrounding the legend of Robin Hood, differs sharply from the Dwan-Fairbanks silent version of 1922, much to the

THE PERFECT SPECIMEN (1937). With Joan Blondell

THE ADVENTURES OF ROBIN HOOD (1938). With Olivia de Havilland

later version's advantage. The silent film is static and interminable, its pomp and pageantry completely overwhelming the colorful characters and narrative. For the Flynn version, screenwriters Norman Reilly Raine and Seton I. Miller incorporated incidents from everywhere, a little Sir Walter Scott here, a bit from the DeKoven-Smith light opera there. The resulting film brims over with a richness of detail and an eye for character rare in such storybook narratives.

The basic narrative chronicles the Saxon knight, Sir Robin of Locksley's reprisals against the Norman trio of cutthroats, Prince John, Sir Guy of Gisbourne, and the Sheriff of Nottingham, who have usurped the rule of England in the absence of King Richard the Lionhearted, held captive by the Austrians on his return from the Third Crusade in Palestine. Within this framework, most of the favorite tales surrounding the legend of Robin Hood are introduced. The bout with quarterstaves between Little John and Robin Hood on a log spanning a stream is robustly performed by Alan Hale and Flynn. Eugene Pallette, one of the most lovable character actors in American films, is a marvelous Friar Tuck, and his first encounter with the outlaw of Sherwood Forest begins with Flynn's riding him piggyback into the water and ends shortly thereafter in a midstream fencing duel. Maid Marian figures prominently in the action, of course, and the love scenes between Olivia de Havilland and Flynn have a romantic intensity unsurpassed in their Curtiz films together. Their scene in Maid Marian's chambers near the end of the film, with Flynn climbing up the vines outside her wall to join her on her balcony, is truly inspired, the tenderness and passion of their playing beautifully complemented by Erich Wolfgang Korngold's haunting love theme.

Although William Keighley and Michael Curtiz both receive credit for the direction, *The Adventures of Robin Hood* has the look and feel of a Curtiz epic. The vigor of the many action set pieces can certainly be attributed to Curtiz. Robin Hood's merry men cascading out of oaks and sycamores onto Norman caravans, Robin Hood's incredible escape from Nottingham Castle near the beginning of the film, and the final sequence beginning with the "monks'" procession to Prince John's coronation and culminating in the exemplary duel between Basil Rathbone and Flynn—all bear the unmistakable stamp of Curtiz. The duel is one of the most exciting ever filmed, and is replete with Curtiz touches—overturned candelabra, the duelers' shadows reflected on an enormous pillar in the foreground of the image, a dramat-

THE ADVENTURES OF ROBIN HOOD (1938). With Basil Rathbone

THE ADVENTURES OF ROBIN HOOD (1938). Robin is dubbed a knight by Richard (Ian Hunter) as Maid Marian (Olivia de Havilland) and the "merry men" look on.

ically employed winding staircase, and numerous close-ups of the opponents locking blades.

There are many elements that make *Robin Hood* one of the quintessential adventure films for children of all ages. The sweeping score by Erich Wolfgang Korngold, almost operatic in its density of themes and Wagnerian passion; the brilliant use of three-strip Technicolor, with dark browns and greens dominating the Sherwood Forest sequences and vibrant reds and purples in the castle interiors; and Sol Polito and Tony Gaudio's expressionistic photography, with its reliance on heavily accented areas of light and shadow—all contribute to an example of the Hollywood cinema at its finest.

Ultimately, the greatest triumph of *Robin Hood* belongs to Flynn. He is the propelling energy behind the robust high spirits pervading every scene. The picture of self-confidence and athletic vitality, Flynn is never stationary in this film. Even when he's not climbing up parapets or swinging on sycamore vines, his body appears to be in perpetual motion. Never has he looked so dashing, fenced with such dexterity, or moved with such agil-

FOUR'S A CROWD (1938). With Rosalind Russell

ity. The ingratiating mixture of chivalrous gallantry and roguish impudence that defines his persona is in rich display here. The manner in which he strides into a royal banquet, a deer slung across his back, and then proceeds to deposit the dead animal onto the banquet table, is a joy to behold. The rebelliousness against authority and corruption that shaped his early screen image finds perfect expression in the merry outlaw who steals from the rich to give to the poor. His infinite tenderness toward de Havilland, his joviality with Hale and Pallette, and the jaunty insolence with which he confronts Rathbone and Claude Rains are all colorful aspects of a larger-than-life performance. Until Raoul Walsh began to explore the Flynn persona and delve into the darker underside of the dashing adventurer image, *Robin Hood* remained the most perfect meeting of star and role to emerge from the Flynn-Curtiz years.

Flynn's performances in his three other 1938 films stand in sharp contrast to Robin Hood. *Four's a Crowd* is another Curtiz attempt at light comedy in which Flynn, Olivia de Havilland, Rosalind Russell, and Patric Knowles perform a singularly unamusing *pas de quatre*, with Flynn as an ambitious publicity man, de Havilland as a flighty debutante, Russell as an aggressive newspaper reporter, and Knowles as her publisher. In the unlikely denouement, Flynn pairs off with Russell, who proves particularly abrasive in one of the earliest incarnations of the emasculating female she was to hone to perfection over the next decade. (The film's one bright spot is Walter Connolly as de Havilland's eccentric grandfather.)

Flynn's next 1938 film, *The Sisters*, was designed primarily as another tear-drenched vehicle for Bette Davis, but the actor *did* receive top billing, and his role is the most complex and interesting in the film. He plays an irresponsible sportswriter from San Francisco who spirits the smitten Davis away from her small-town family, ensconces her in a cold-water flat in the Bay City, and proceeds to drink his life away. Perhaps the fact that the role contains elements of Flynn's own self-destructive personality accounts for the fascination of his performance. The actor's dissipation as the film progresses assumes existential overtones, and the obligatory happy ending does not relieve the aura of despair his character casts over the second half of the film.

In other respects, *The Sisters* is a competent enough tearjerker. Anatole Litvak films much of it with real style, particularly the opening sequences which beautifully convey the closeness of Davis to her family, and the rupture created within this

THE SISTERS (1938). With Bette Davis

unit by her elopement with Flynn. Once the couple get to San Francisco, however, the structure of the film falls apart. Litvak inadequately develops the implied parallels among Davis and her two sisters' marriages, and by the time the film's *piece de resistance*—the 1906 earthquake—arrives, the film has more or less evaporated.

John Monk Saunders and Howard Hawks' original story, "Flight Commander," had been the basis for Hawks' first sound film, *The Dawn Patrol*, in 1930. Warners decided to remake this vintage tale in 1938 with Edmund Goulding directing, and Flynn, Basil Rathbone, and David Niven in the roles created by Richard Barthelmess,

THE SISTERS (1938). With Bette Davis

Neil Hamilton, and Douglas Fairbanks, Jr. (Raoul Walsh filmed the same plot in 1948 under the title, *Fighter Squadron*). The lasting appeal of *The Dawn Patrol* is its classic elements of men in war, their camaraderie, their devotion to duty, their tension under conflict, and their courage and stoicism in the face of death.

During World War I, the 59th Squadron of the British Royal Flying Corps is retaliating against German aircraft advances in France. The squadron's flights against the Germans begin at dawn and usually involve heavy losses. Even though the squadron commander (Rathbone) undergoes living hell each time he sends his men on one of these missions, the outcome of which is always doubtful, ace pilot Flynn is highly critical of the seemingly random relegation of so many young boys to certain death. When Rathbone is promoted because of an unauthorized mission flown by Flynn and Niven that demolishes an enemy outpost, he appoints Flynn as the new squadron commander.

Flynn is now a rebel faced with responsibility, and he soon begins to experience the same moral dilemma and mental anguish that had all but unhinged Rathbone. When Niven's younger brother, a raw recruit to the "dawn patrol," is shot down over enemy lines, Niven turns against his former best friend, and Flynn begins to drink heavily.

THE DAWN PATROL (1938). With David Niven, Donald Crisp, and Basil Rathbone

THE DAWN PATROL (1938). With David Niven and Michael Brooke

Hoping to redeem himself in the eyes of his old buddy, Flynn gets Niven drunk and takes his place on a suicide mission to destroy a German ammunition dump. As the film ends, we see Niven assuming the rank of squadron commander.

Goulding is not the ideal director for such material, his rather limited talents being much more suited to the facile slickness of *The Great Lie* or *Dark Victory*. His inability to render the action sequences effectively was apparently realized early on by the studio, as most of the flying footage is recycled stock from the Hawks version. Goulding is somewhat more successful in his handling of the more intimate scenes in the club bar of the Fliers' headquarters, and he is aided considerably by the sympathetic performances of Niven and Flynn, who display an extraordinary rapport in their scenes together.

Flynn's performance in *The Dawn Patrol* is one of his most affecting around this period in his career. He often plays against the mood of a particular scene, enriching the effect with contrast and a sense of irony. An affectionate smile lingers on his face as he describes the horror of Niven's supposed death to Rathbone. He comforts a jittery recruit whose friend has just been killed in action, the nervous smoking of a cigarette belying his calm manner and soothing speech. The scene in which Rathbone returns to headquarters with the orders for the volunteer suicide mission is Flynn's most inventive in the film. The alcohol to which the pressures of flight commander have driven him produces an almost offhand reaction to Rathbone's orders. Flynn looks just beyond Rathbone during this scene; he seems to be listening to a voice he alone can hear. The drinking is subtly integrated into the characterization, underscored by the frequency with which Flynn refills his glass. Flynn's playing of this scene is quirky, neurotic, and disturbing; it is also tinged with an excitement that the actor rarely brought to his more introspective roles.

1939 was the year of the epic Western, and none was more spectacular than *Dodge City*, the vehicle Warner Bros. designed around Errol Flynn. If most of these Westerns lacked nothing in the way of sweep and spectacle, they were diminished somewhat by the comic-strip narratives and the one-dimensional characters that filled the pauses between large action set pieces.

Dodge City was Flynn's first Western, and director Michael Curtiz was careful to embellish his role with the dash and bravura audiences had come to expect in the actor's swashbucklers. Flynn portrayed Wade Hatton, a soldier-of-fortune who, upon completion of the railroad into Dodge City, hires on as a trail boss. The coming of the railroad precipitates an outbreak of lawlessness and corruption in Dodge City, epitomized by crooked cattle deals, unscrupulous gambling dens, and nefarious palaces of booze and sin. Most of the townspeople urge Flynn to accept the job of sheriff, but he hesitates until the small son of a man who has been killed by the local mob is himself killed by runaway horses, excited by the gunshots of local riffraff outside the saloon. Flynn becomes sheriff, eradicates the venal trio who have controlled the town, and brings about reform and change through the use

THE PEAK YEARS: ON LAND, AT SEA, IN THE AIR

of the local newspaper. He leaves with his bride, Olivia de Havilland, to tame another raw frontier outpost, Virginia City.

Curtiz keeps everything moving so fast that one scarcely notices the lack of depth in the script and the paucity of characterization. His surly trio of villains—Bruce Cabot, Victor Jory, and Douglas Fowley—is beautifully balanced by the three "good guys," Flynn, Guinn "Big Boy" Williams, and Alan Hale. The film is loaded with action highlights —an exciting race between stagecoach and train gets the film off to a rollicking start. The most famous set piece in the film, and justifiably so, is the saloon brawl that erupts midway in the film, a sequence in which Flynn does not even appear.

In his first Western, Flynn looks a bit uncomfortable in the opening scenes of the film, but by the time he rescues de Havilland from a burning mail car on the Dodge City train, he has become thoroughly assimilated into the genre which was to serve him well during his career. Flynn's Wade Hatton is an engaging and temperate protagonist, a man who has an innate integrity as well as no small amount of

47

self-interest. The crucial moment in the film for Flynn is the death of the young boy. It is here that Flynn decides to assume the job of sheriff, and as he jumps on his horse in a futile attempt to rescue the boy, Curtiz tracks away from horse and rider in an exhilarating shot that gives us the essence of Flynn as an adventurer of integrity and honor.

As in all of their films together, *Dodge City* features many lovely moments of interplay between Flynn and de Havilland, none more engaging perhaps than the scene on a hill in the country outside Dodge City where Flynn boldly courts his ladylove as she stubbornly, but never too seriously, resists his undeniable charms.

Dodge City was a phenomenal success at the box office, and catapulted Flynn into one of the Top Ten Stars of 1939. He was at the pinnacle of his career, and Warners seldom let him rest for long between assignments. He was immediately cast opposite Bette Davis again in one of the studio's "prestige" properties, *The Private Lives of Elizabeth and Essex.* There was much off-camera animosity between the two stars. Davis had wanted Laurence Olivier to play Essex. She had also just been through a hassle with Jack Warner; the intrepid producer had offered Flynn and her in a package to David O. Selznick for *Gone With the Wind.* Davis balked at the proposal, primarily because she had little regard for Flynn's abilities as an actor.

The antipathy between the pair is ill-concealed on the screen. Even in *The Sisters,* the two performers had communicated little rapport toward one another. In their second teaming, the friction between them encumbers an already leaden drama, rendering it as cold and frigid as the Virgin Queen herself.

Based on Maxwell Anderson's *Elizabeth the Queen, The Private Lives of Elizabeth and Essex* emerges as a series of lifeless tableaux, sporadically brought to life by a bit of incidental pageantry or one of director Michael Curtiz's expressionistic flourishes. Davis becomes almost a parody of herself in the mirror-smashing sequence, her performance comprised mostly of predictable mannerisms and the elaborate, external accoutrements of her characterization—the red wig, the powdered face, and her tiny figure encased in high lace collar and Catherine wheel.

Next to his co-star's pyrotechnics, Flynn seems rather diminutive and lost. Perhaps the actor was intimidated by the knowledge that he was not wanted by his formidable leading lady. In any case, the performance is colorless and lackluster. The ardor he declares for his queen throughout the film is scarcely

DODGE CITY (1939). As Wade Hatton

DODGE CITY (1939). With Olivia de Havilland

THE PRIVATE LIVES OF ELIZABETH AND ESSEX (1939). With Bette Davis

believable, and the lack of tension between the two undercuts the basic dramatic conflict of the narrative.

Flynn does redeem himself somewhat at the end, when he is led to the chopping block, his sandy hair blowing in the wind, the very image of a romantic martyr. As he requests his executioners to untie his hands so that he may kiss the ring his beloved monarch had once given him, the emotional resonance of the film deepens, strengthening the effect of Flynn's glorious delivery of the line, "We could have searched the earth for two such perfect lovers, and ended the search with ourselves."

Eager to cash in on the box-office success of *Dodge City*, Curtiz and Flynn embarked on another Western saga, loosely structured around the name of a sprawling, wide-open frontier town. This time, they called it *Virginia City*.

In terms of character and narrative structure, *Virginia City* is one of the most engrossing films Flynn made under Curtiz. Set against the raging conflict of the Civil War, the film presents three characters—Flynn, Miriam Hopkins, and Randolph Scott—whose interests and loyalties are continually shifting throughout the course of the film.

Flynn again plays a soldier-of-fortune, one of the leading sources of enemy intelligence who, at the beginning of the film, is incarcerated in a Union prison camp. The prisoners are treated as savages, ruled over by a true Curtiz sadist, Randolph Scott.

In a last desperate effort to save the South, Scott's childhood sweetheart, Hopkins, tells him of five million dollars in gold bullion waiting in Virginia City to salvage the bankrupt Confederacy. Flynn escapes about the same time that Scott and Hopkins head separately for Virginia City, and the Union enlists his aid in preventing the gold's falling into Confederate hands. As the three characters converge on Virginia City, their lives cross and intertwine, lending the latter portions of the film a tone of disturbing ambiguity.

Flynn is persuasive in yet another variation on the adventurer image he had now perfected under Curtiz's astute direction. His wooing of Hopkins (ludicrously miscast as a saloon thrush, and unflatteringly photographed to boot) has all of the Flynn stocks-in-trade—exaggerated heroics and much romantic prattle of predestination and destiny, with just the right hint of wild mischief underlying all the passionate declarations.

Curtiz's direction is a cut above his usual yeomanlike job. One of those sublime moments, indigenous to films, occurs when Flynn visits the Sazerac Saloon on his arrival in Virginia City. The realization that the "lady" he courted on the stagecoach is a dance-hall girl reverberates so powerfully that a few short moments later, when Scott walks into the saloon and sees Flynn and Hopkins reflected in the large mirror over the bar, the effect is truly extraordinary. A complex network of human relationships and behavior has been evoked primarily through visual associations and connections.

Curtiz also utilizes the landscape expressively when the action moves out of Virginia City, and the journey with the gold begins. If it were not for the unsympathetic performance of Hopkins and Humphrey Bogart's poor performance as an incredibly accented Mexican bandit, *Virginia City* would rank even higher as one of Flynn's most memorable films.

Flynn's second film in 1940 was *The Sea Hawk*, another Sabatini property Warners dusted off in the hopes of recapturing the success of *Captain Blood*. First National had filmed a silent version of the novel in 1924 with Milton Sills, but the script eventually used for the remake underwent a series of metamorphoses before it reached the screen. Delmer Daves worked on

THE PRIVATE LIVES OF ELIZABETH AND ESSEX (1939). Essex being led to his execution

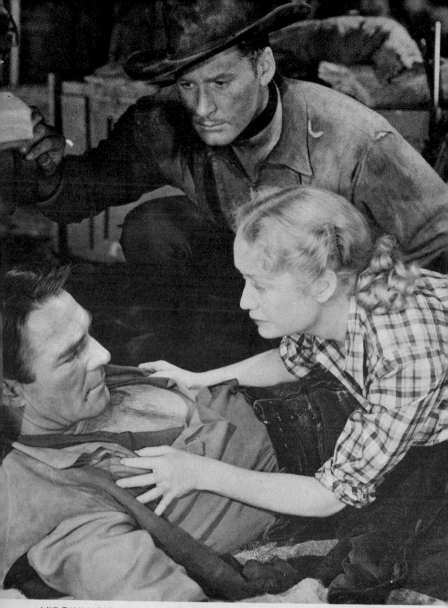
VIRGINIA CITY (1940). With Randolph Scott and Miriam Hopkins

VIRGINIA CITY (1940). With Randolph Scott

the first adaptation for the studio, but his work was scrapped. Howard Koch, the author of Orson Welles' "War of the Worlds" radio broadcast, was hired by Warners to revise a screenplay by Seton I. Miller, dealing with the exploits of an adventurer who was loosely based on Sir Francis Drake. Little of Sabatini's novel remains in Koch's final script, and the character Flynn portrays bears more than a passing resemblance to the real-life Drake.

Warners' faith in the property was justified. *The Sea Hawk* is, in many respects, a glorious adventure film, and apart from *Robin Hood*, showcases Flynn at his swashbuckling peak.

Flynn is Captain Geoffrey Thorpe, the commander of a band of privateers who engage in marauding expeditions against Spanish treasure ships. Although these "sea hawks" are, in effect, waging an undeclared war on the

THE SEA HAWK (1940). With David Bruce and Alan Hale

Spanish Armada, Thorpe has the private—if not the public—sanction of Queen Elizabeth (Flora Robson) for these expeditions. A trip to Panama to raid a treasure train in the jungle backfires, and Thorpe and his men are sentenced by the Spanish Inquisition to serve as galley slaves aboard a Spanish galleon. They manage to escape in time, however, to warn Queen Elizabeth of the Spanish Armada's plans to attack England, and to oust a spy (Henry Daniell), who has infiltrated the court to inform the Spanish against the queen.

The one real flaw in *The Sea Hawk* is the tenuous motivation underlying Flynn's daredevil actions throughout the film. Flynn

THE SEA HAWK (1940). Geoffrey Thorpe is dubbed a knight by Queen Elizabeth (Flora Robson).

ostensibly subjects himself to all sorts of danger and suffering during the course of the film, as a result of his great respect and unspoken love for the queen of England. These reasons, however, hardly seem commensurate with what we are actually shown on the screen. The one long scene between Flynn and Flora Robson's superbly enacted Queen Elizabeth, as magnificent as it is, must supply the impetus for Flynn's subsequent actions, and that seems an inordinate amount of weight for one scene to support. Since the explication of their relationship is ephemeral at best, the film often resembles a series of spectacular set pieces, albeit brilliantly done.

Another weakness in the film is Flynn's co-star, Brenda Marshall. Although her part is admittedly small, in retrospect it seems even thinner, because she literally makes no impression at all.

Given these shortcomings, *The Sea Hawk* is still great fun on its own terms. Curtiz was once again at the helm, and he keeps the narrative moving at his usual brisk pace. The somewhat overripe Korngold score often seems to be shaping the visuals, rather than complementing them, but it does effectively underscore such memorable moments as the opening battle between English and Spanish vessels, the surreal aspects of the men's entrapment in the swamps of Panama, and the violent uprising of the oarsmen aboard the Spanish galleon.

Flynn romps through *The Sea Hawk*, obviously having the time of his life. At the time of the film's release, he was bemoaning to reporters the fact that he was tired of being typecast in swashbucklers, and that he longed to do more "serious" roles which would challenge his capabilities as an actor. No evidence of this dissatisfaction can be found in his performance, however; it is one of his most ingratiating and invigorating characterizations.

Flynn incorporates all of the elements that make up his screen image into the role of Captain Geoffrey Thorpe. He is saucy and impudent in his repartée with Robson, chivalrous and ardent in his romancing of Marshall, gallant in his treatment of the women he takes as prisoners, and bold and defiant when confronting his enemies, whether he is swinging from the rigging of his magnificent vessel, or engaging the arch-villain (Daniell) in a duel to the death. This obligatory duel, which is the actual climax to a film that is made up almost entirely of climactic moments, assumes almost delirious proportions, even for Curtiz. It ranges through almost every room in the castle, and the shadows of the two opponents are seen more frequently than the men themselves. Many of Curtiz's visual

*SANTA FE TRAIL (1940). With Ronald Reagan
and William Lundigan*

effects in this film seem a bit too grandiose, especially in the absence of the personalization of character and narrative that would support such flourishes.

Flynn teamed with Curtiz again in 1940 for *Santa Fe Trail*, another historical Western with an epic structure, this time centered on the events and incidents surrounding

SANTA FE TRAIL (1940). With Ronald Reagan and Olivia de Havilland

the rise and fall of the fanatic abolitionist, John Brown. One may undergo a feeling of *déjà vu* while watching *Santa Fe Trail*. Curtiz reuses anything that seemed to work for him in *Dodge City* and *Virginia City*. Alan Hale and Guinn "Big Boy" Williams are on hand again as Flynn's comic sidekicks. (At one point, they try to barbecue an unskinned cow.) As in the two earlier Westerns, an innocent young boy loses his life as a result of the rampant villainy. Fortunately, however, Olivia de Havilland returns as a welcome replacement for Miriam Hopkins.

It is ironic that in *Virginia City*, made the same year, the characters and their relationships are so interesting and sharply focused, whereas the historical elements are blurred and rather vague. The exact opposite is true of *Santa Fe Trail*. The historical background of the later film is sharp and precise, but the more intimate elements involving Flynn and de Havilland are soft and undefined. The film's balance is made even more precarious by the intensity of every scene in the film that deals with the character of John Brown. Raymond Massey's demonic performance dominates the film, and Curtiz supports the performance with elaborate flourishes of theatrical expressionism. The visual highlight of the film comes when Massey delivers his "sword of Jehovah" speech atop a hill as his hideaway burns in the distance, the gnarled branches of trees forming a gaunt framework for the obsessed figure praying on his knees.

Flynn strides through his one-dimensional role in amiable fashion, but it is one of his least exciting performances around this time.

Although Flynn revealed a distinct flair for light comedy in many of his swashbucklers and action films, the few real comedies in which he appeared failed to develop his potential in this vein. *Footsteps in the Dark*, a mystery-farce of the *Thin Man* school, is one of the actor's dreariest vehicles. Flynn plays a man-about-town who doubles as a detective. The only remotely amusing aspects of this purported comedy are Lee Patrick's energetic performance as a hard-boiled stripper and the idea, in theory if not in execution, of Ralph Bellamy as a dentist who also happens to be a murderer.

Dive Bomber was Flynn's twelfth and last film under the direction of Michael Curtiz. It was widely rumored at the time that Flynn was rebelling against the strenuous working conditions that prevailed on a Curtiz set. Curtiz was a hard-driving perfectionist and perhaps Flynn, at the peak of his stardom, desired a more relaxed working atmosphere.

Flynn looks quite relaxed himself

FOOTSTEPS IN THE DARK (1941). With Lee Patrick

in *Dive Bomber*, one of many bland movies churned out by the studios on the eve of America's entry into World War II. Even as war-thumping propaganda, the film isn't very effective. By far the most ineffectual collaboration between Curtiz and Flynn, *Dive Bomber*'s only asset is the breathtakingly beautiful aerial photography, shot in ripe forties Technicolor by Elmer Dyer and Charles Marshall. Flynn played a naval surgeon who becomes interested in aviation medicine and proves his heroism after being bitterly resented by the men he commands.

Also in 1941, Errol Flynn starred in his first film directed by Raoul Walsh. Walsh was to direct the actor in seven films over a period of seven years. Their collaboration produced the richest exploration of the Flynn persona. Flynn displays many facets under Walsh; his performances under this director are charged with a vitality and an inner rhythm that are absent in even the best of the Curtiz films. Walsh reveals a vulnerability in Flynn that gives his bold adventurer image the leavening qualities of pathos and humanity. Perhaps the fact that the two men were close friends contributed to a relaxed, cooperative working relationship.

DIVE BOMBER (1941). With Fred MacMurray and Ralph Bellamy

THEY DIED WITH THEIR BOOTS ON (1941). With Olivia de Havilland

Besides being a magnificent showcase for one of Flynn's most bravura performances, *They Died with Their Boots On* is a spectacular achievement on any level. Obviously patterned after the enormously successful *Charge of the Light Brigade,* the later film is its superior in every way. Although Walsh romanticizes the legend of General George Armstrong Custer, there is enough ego and vanity in Flynn's portrayal to lend a double edge to the film. *They Died with Their Boots On* is neither as whitewashed a presentation of Custer nor as simplistic a view of the historical events surrounding this colorful figure as it may appear at a casual viewing. The film has a headlong tragic thrust that culminates in the massive Last Stand at the Little Big Horn, one of the greatest action set pieces in the history of the movies.

Flynn gives one of his finest performances as the brash young West Point cadet who forges a legend out of his experiences in the Civil War and against the Sioux and Cheyenne. He flamboyantly enters the film astride a horse, an elegant dandy of a figure complete with plumed hat and trailed by a little black boy tending his hounds. This swaggering image of braggadocio is brought down to earth by his nemesis (Arthur Kennedy), in the first of a series of private skirmishes that will punctuate his career throughout the film. Flynn's ego is continually being subverted by other characters—Kennedy's Ned Sharp, Anthony Quinn's Crazy Horse, Stanley Ridges' devious Major Taipe, and in gentler ways, by his wife, Olivia de Havilland.

Flynn is a true Walsh adventurer, plunging into the unknown just for the sheer thrill of the adventure itself. In the action sequences, Flynn assumes the vulnerability of so many Walsh protagonists rushing tragically toward death. The inactivity that comes at the close of the Civil War finds him at a loss; he drinks in town all day, reliving the glory of his battles and living off his wife's estate. Through the intervention of his wife, Flynn is given command of the Seventh Cavalry in the Dakota Territory. The aggressive West Point rebel becomes the sternest disciplinarian; to the montage-modulated tune of "Garry Owen," he whips the Seventh into fighting shape.

Flynn's singular concern with himself undergoes a process of change. Through his deepening awareness of the sacrifices his wife has made for his happiness, and his realization of the brutal treatment the Indians are receiving at the hands of the U.S. government, Flynn's ego and pride begin to be placed in a more rational perspective, clearing the way for his final, tragic sacrifice.

*THEY DIED WITH THEIR BOOTS ON (1941). With Gene Lockhart and
Olivia de Havilland*

THEY DIED WITH THEIR BOOTS ON (1941). With Charley Grapewin

They Died with Their Boots On is the eighth and last film Flynn made with Olivia de Havilland. Their final scene, when Custer is preparing to embark on the suicide mission to the Little Big Horn, is charged with emotional resonance. The scene boasts some of the finest acting either star has ever done. When Flynn says to his wife, "Walking through life with you, ma'am, has been a very gracious thing, indeed," the passionate kiss that follows achieves a rapturous lyricism. As Flynn walks out of the room, Walsh's camera tracks after him, seeming to *will* him to stay in the room with her. The next shot tracks away from the isolated figure of de Havilland, emphasizing her aloneness, her faint providing the period to this remarkable passage, one of the loveliest in Walsh's films.

The year 1942 was a turning point in Flynn's personal life. His first wife, Lili Damita, divorced him, he was acquitted of statutory rape in a highly publicized trial (which, if anything, tripled his box-office draw), and he met his second wife, Nora Eddington, who was working at the cigar counter in the Los Angeles Hall of Justice during the rape trial. The couple was to have two children, Deirdre and Rory, before divorcing in 1949.

Flynn's 1942 releases, *Desperate Journey* and *Gentleman Jim*, continued his relationship with director Raoul Walsh. *Desperate Journey* is a mile-a-minute recounting of a five-man invasion of Nazi Germany. Flynn plays an Australian flight lieutenant in the RAF, commissioned to bomb a network of factories in Germany. Accompanying Flynn on the mission are such composite types as Arthur Kennedy's thoughtful Canadian, Alan Hale's lovable Scot, Ronald Reagan's gung-ho American ("half-American, half-Jersey City"), and the sacrificial lamb of the group, Ronald Sinclair.

Desperate Journey adds to Walsh's exploration of the darker side of Flynn's Napoleonic image. The director questions the actions of this bold adventurer throughout the film. For instance, Flynn ignores strict orders to remain at a high altitude during the bombing, flying far too low and being shot down on enemy soil, losing three of his crew in the process.

Once they are shot down, Flynn continues to throw caution to the wind by undertaking the diversionary tactic of demolishing a vital chemical plant in Berlin. The more responsible Kennedy urges Flynn to concern himself with getting the group back to Allied territory with the valuable information they have taken from Nazi major Raymond Massey's headquarters. Flynn's relentless thirst for adventure, reckless and irresponsible as it is, thrusts aside Kennedy's protestations, further endangering the lives of his cohorts, and actually resulting in the deaths of Sinclair and Hale. The implication that Flynn's hell-bent desire to leave "a couple of bouquets" behind is the cause of his friends' deaths darkens the character and lends disturbing overtones to the Boy Scout maneuvers of the invading team.

The excellence of *Desperate Journey* lies in Walsh's ability to convey these multiple meanings in a film that barely pauses long enough to catch its breath. Quite possibly the *fastest* movie ever

DESPERATE JOURNEY (1942). With Ronald Reagan, Arthur Kennedy, and Alan Hale

made, *Desperate Journey* takes the term "action for action's sake" and turns it into a profound way of looking at its wartime milieu.

Gentleman Jim is the most satisfying and entertaining of Raoul Walsh's seven films with Errol Flynn. Moreover, it is in this electric, kinetic performance that the quintessential Flynn emerges. If one film had to be selected to illustrate the qualities that made Flynn a star, *Gentleman Jim* would be the one. The unharnessed energy, the combination of naïveté and aggressiveness, the bold charm, the elegant virility—all the Flynn charac-

teristics receive their richest expression in his embodiment of James J. Corbett.

Flynn emerges in *Gentleman Jim* as one of the purest incarnations of the Walsh hero, that breed of man who pursues adventure just for the hell of it. Flynn's Corbett plunges headlong into boxing simply because it seems more exciting and stimulating than remaining a bank teller for the rest of his life. The character's unquenchable thirst for excitement, his impulsive behavior that would border on the neurotic if Walsh had opted for a darker treatment, finds its visual correlative in

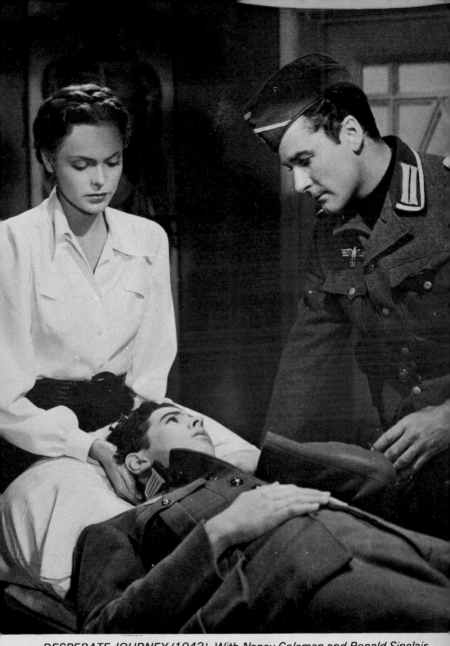

DESPERATE JOURNEY (1942). With Nancy Coleman and Ronald Sinclair

the pell-mell pace at which Walsh has directed the film. *Gentleman Jim* hurls forward at a dizzying pace, culminating in the final bout for the boxing championship of the world between Corbett and John L. Sullivan, a sequence that leaves the viewer as breathless as it does the participants and the crowds in the film.

Like its hero, *Gentleman Jim* finds its *raison d'être* in physical movement. The choreographed elegance of the men doing their exercises in the gym at the fashionable club to which Flynn aspires; the bouts themselves, especially the fight by the river in the central section of the film, which has high-angle shots of the crowd, ring, water, and lights, alternating with close shots of Flynn and his opponent; and the total physicality of Flynn's performance, all contribute a physical energy and delirious frenzy reminiscent of Jean Renoir's *French Can-Can.*

Flynn's gem of a performance is beautifully supported by Alan Hale in one of his greatest roles as Corbett's Irish rogue of a father, Ward Bond as John L. Sullivan, whose ego and bluster almost match his brash young opponent's, and

GENTLEMAN JIM (1942). With William Frawley and Alexis Smith

GENTLEMAN JIM (1942). With Lynne Roberts and Alexis Smith

GENTLEMAN JIM (1942). With Rhys Williams (referee)

Alexis Smith, looking sleek and lovely if not exactly animated, as Flynn's sparring partner in the romantic department. The picture belongs to Flynn, however; and near the end of the film, Walsh strips his protagonist of the proud defenses that have propelled him into the boxing championship of the world, once again allowing us to see a softer, more vulnerable aspect of the Flynn persona. Bond visits Flynn's post-victory party to acknowledge this fresh upstart's assumption of the title of new world's champion. The playing between the two actors is nothing less than sublime, and as Bond's ex-champ is seen leaving the party, his defeated but proud image reflected in a mirror next to Flynn, one is again struck by the depth of compassion that marks Raoul Walsh as one of the screen's greatest humanists.

Flynn's 4-F draft rating kept him out of World War II, but a glance at the films he made during this period makes it appear as though this virile Australian won the war single-handedly. Warner Bros. kept him busy constantly; even when the notoriety of the rape trial was at its peak, Flynn continued to make movies. When he was not in court or before the camera, the actor could be found most often on his ketch, the *Sirocco*, named after the schooner he had owned in Australia. The lure of the sea continued to exert its hold on Flynn.

Flynn is a man of the sea once again in *Edge of Darkness* (1943), in which he plays the fisherman leader of the underground in an occupied Norwegian village. Directed with stodgy didacticism by Lewis Milestone, the film is a fitting companion piece to the director's *North Star*, released the same year. The film's portentous and mechanical style perfectly complements screenwriter Robert Rossen's simplistic tract on good and evil.

Flynn's role is vague and undeveloped. The film is conceived as an ensemble piece, and most of the meatier parts are in the hands of such capable supporting actors as Walter Huston, Judith Anderson, and Morris Carnovsky. Ruth Gordon is particularly outstanding as Huston's wife, a woman on the verge of breakdown at the disruption of her family and her way of life. Helmut Dantine gives his ultimate Nazi imitation as the commander of a garrison where all of his own men loathe him.

The film has the look and feel of mere propaganda, and bad propaganda at that. One of director Milestone's "subtler" touches is his treatment of Ann Sheridan's rape by a Nazi soldier who has been eyeing her all through the film. As she leaves the church (an appropriate setting), Milestone photographs only her legs. The leg of the Nazi

EDGE OF DARKNESS (1943). With Walter Huston

EDGE OF DARKNESS (1943). With Walter Huston and Ann Sheridan

soldier reaches out to trip her, and then the camera moves outside the church, catching the lower anatomy of marching patrols, then craning upward to include the cross over the entrance to the church.

This type of self-conscious symbolism infiltrates the characters' dialogue as well. *Edge of Darkness* is one of those movies where every character is *terribly* aware of the larger meaning of the situation. Each villager seems assured of his eventual niche in eternity. When this aborted allegory meets Milestone's academic direction, the result is a deadly bore.

Flynn next sang and danced "That's What You Jolly Well Get" in *Thank Your Lucky Stars*, Warner

*THANK YOUR LUCKY STARS (1943). Singing "That's What You
Jolly Well Get"*

Bros.' entry in the all-star musical cavalcades so popular with moviegoers during the war. His deft handling of the Frank Loesser-Arthur Schwartz song makes one wish he had been given a full-length musical role. The fact that he almost dances through *Gentleman Jim* is further proof that Flynn might have really excelled in the genre.

For *Northern Pursuit*, his last film in 1943, Flynn was reunited with director Raoul Walsh. Arguably the weakest collaboration between the two, *Northern Pursuit* is nevertheless a fascinating continuation of Walsh's penetration of the Flynn image.

Flynn is a German-born member of the Royal Canadian Mounted Police who fakes defection in order to infiltrate a group of Nazi saboteurs determined to bomb one of the most vital water arteries connecting the United States and Canada. As in *Desperate Journey*, the lives of others are jeopardized by Flynn's actions. For instance, his deception endangers the life of his fiancée and results in the cold-blooded killing of fellow mountie John Ridgely by the Nazis. At one point in the film Flynn's nemesis (Helmut Dantine in a performance of obsessive power), the leader of the group of saboteurs, accuses Flynn of endangering the lives of those closest to him through his actions, and Walsh dollies in to an anguished close-up of Flynn's face, holding it there as the implication of guilt plays over his features.

Although *Northern Pursuit* lacks the intensity and force of Walsh's best films, it still moves as swiftly as lightning and has more than its share of exciting action sequences. The opening of the film is almost surreal, as a German submarine eerily rises out of the icy Canadian waters. Dantine's escape from the internment camp is also memorably staged, an electrifying montage of escaping figures amidst the snow, barbed wire, and searchlights.

Flynn's love interest in the film is the pallid Julie Bishop. Apparently, even the scenarists didn't take their relationship too seriously, because in the final scene, right after they've been married, she simpers: "Am I the only girl you ever really loved?" Flynn retorts, "Why, of course you are, darling," embraces her, then confides to the camera with a look of astonishment, "What am I saying?" This ending must have convulsed audiences at the time, coming as it did in Flynn's first movie to be released after he had been acquitted for rape.

Only one Flynn film was released in 1944, but it contained one of the most unsettling roles of his career. Jean Picard in *Uncertain Glory* emerges as one of the most fascinating characters in the gallery of Flynn portrayals. Picard is a petty

NORTHERN PURSUIT (1943). With Helmut Dantine (in left foreground)

thief, a specialist in blackmail, forgery, and burglary, who is about to be guillotined for the murder of a night watchman that occurred during a jewelry store robbery. When an air raid over Paris provides cover for Picard's escape, his nemesis (Paul Lukas) chases him to the Spanish border, recaptures him, and the two men embark on the return trip to Paris. When the train is rerouted because three saboteurs have dynamited a German convoy, Picard pleads with the French detective to allow him to confess to the crime, preferring a German firing squad to the guillotine. In the process he can also save one hundred French hostages who will be executed by the Germans if the saboteurs refuse to surrender. Picard makes his thrust at martyr-

UNCERTAIN GLORY (1944). With Faye Emerson

dom initially to stave off execution for a day or so, but his relationships with Lukas and a young French country girl (Jean Sullivan) transform his cynicism into honor, and his detachment from the maelstrom of World War II into an oblique form of patriotism.

Inconsistencies in the script lessen the credibility of Flynn's transformation, but director Raoul Walsh is able to suggest a great deal by the interchangeable relationship he sets up between Flynn and Lukas, and the almost spiritual tone the scenes with the girl achieve. Flynn is truly remarkable in a role that works against his accustomed image. The charm implicit in his personality gives a dark undercurrent to one of the most amoral characters he ever played. Jean Picard is a desperate convict, playing for time in a relentless cat-and-mouse game with this strange detective who is so obsessed with his capture and arrest.

Flynn has no scruples. Calling on a friend in the French underworld to help him escape, Flynn has no compunctions about helping himself to the man's best suit and his girlfriend as well. He seduces the village girl as a mere peccadillo, even though later his deepening affection for her alters the course of his life.

Flynn has two superb moments in the film. The first occurs when he convinces the ailing Lukas that he wants to confess to the village priest before he dies. The speech is a ruse to enable Flynn to get away from Lukas. Flynn's rendering of it is sincere and honest, totally free of any indications to the audience that his impassioned pleas are merely more lies. The effect is even more devastating when he shuts the door outside, blows a belligerent kiss to the detective within, and bounces jauntily down the stairs, thinking himself to be a free man at last.

Flynn's second outstanding scene occurs in the farmhouse where the girl and he have been given a meal by the parents of one of the hostages about to be executed. As Jean Sullivan lights a candle for the boy, Flynn launches into a tirade against martyrdom and involvement, an assault all the more lacerating because of the identification and empathy we have come to feel for the character.

Walsh is constantly forcing the audience to reexamine its own reactions to the characters and situations in *Uncertain Glory;* the film has an objectivity rare in his films. Coming on the heels of such fast-paced Flynn-Walsh collaborations as *Gentleman Jim* and *Desperate Journey, Uncertain Glory* has an uncharacteristically reflective tone to it. One of the most disturbing films to emerge from Hollywood during World War II, *Uncertain*

UNCERTAIN GLORY (1944). As Jean Picard

OBJECTIVE BURMA (1945). With William Prince and Henry Hull

Glory contains some of the most interesting variations on the Flynn persona. The dark side of the brash adventurer is revealed more clearly than ever before, and a sinister charm that both allures and repels begins to surface, a facet of Flynn that would receive its fullest exploration under Walsh in *Silver River*.

Walsh and Flynn followed *Uncertain Glory* with another winner. *Objective Burma* remains, along with Hawks' *Air Force* and Ford's *They Were Expendable*, one of the three best war films to emerge from the years of World War II. Walsh's film excels in its magnificently staged battle sequences, the diversity and richness of its characters, and the nightmarish intensity of the last third of the film.

Flynn portrays Major Nelson, the leader of a group of American paratroopers dropped into the Burmese jungle to destroy an enemy radar outpost. Once they have accomplished their mission, the film really gets underway. All possibilities of rescue being cut off, Flynn and his men are forced to trek through 150 miles of enemy-filled and disease-infested jungle. The journey becomes as oppressive for the audience as it is for the paratroopers.

James Wong Howe's razor-sharp photography contributes to the documentary feel of the film, an aspect that is reinforced on a narrative level by the presence within the group of a war correspondent (Henry Hull), who goes along to record the realities of war, but ultimately lacks the stamina and fortitude to withstand the pressures of the journey.

Flynn gives one of his most accomplished performances in *Objective Burma*. He is the emotional ballast and moral center of the film, and his group of devoted men as well. It is one of his subtlest, most understated characterizations. There is a real integrity to Flynn's adventurer in this film; he is acutely aware of the responsibilities he has regarding his men, and he is sensitively attuned to their hardships and needs. As he boards the Allied plane carrying him and his survivors to safety at the end of the film, Walsh gives us a close-up of Flynn's face, an expression of loss and regret playing over his features as he recalls the men whose lives were lost on the mission.

The muted affection that Flynn and William Prince as Lieutenant Jacobs display toward one another is unique in that Flynn seldom enters into a close relationship with another male in his films. The ubiquitous Alan Hale and Guinn "Big Boy" Williams act more as buffoons than as real friends. The nearest he comes to such camaraderie is in his

OBJECTIVE BURMA (1945). Leading his men into battle

friendships with Thomas Mitchell and Tom D'Andrea in *Silver River*. Flynn always gives the impression that he has the upper hand; one-to-one relationships with men are rare in his films.

One shot in *Objective Burma* simultaneously captures the essence of both Flynn's adventurer image as well as Walsh's personal attitude toward his adventurer-protagonist. As Flynn stands at the open chute of the airplane, ready to jump into the sky, he becomes the penultimate Walsh adventurer, poised on the edge of the unknown, plunging headlong into adventure once more.

Objective Burma was the center of a storm of controversy at the time of its release. The absence of any British infantry, in a film based on a campaign in which they figured prominently, resulted in the film's being withdrawn from British cinemas. It was finally distributed in England in 1952, with an explanatory prologue tacked on, acknowledging the role the British played in the invasion of Burma.

After *Objective Burma*, the quality of the vehicles in which Flynn appeared decreased sharply. Not only was his box-office power diminishing, but the many years of uninterrupted drinking, drugs, and high living were beginning to take their toll. The increasing frequency with which Flynn walked through his roles did not give him any extra clout to barter for better roles from the studio. His marriage to Nora Eddington ended in 1949, and the actor began spending more and more time away from the screen, sailing his newly acquired schooner, the *Zaca*, to remote ports of call, such as Port Antonio, Jamaica, and Majorca.

In 1946, Flynn published a vaguely autobiographical novel, *Showdown*, which garnered mostly unfavorable reviews. The book dealt with the escapades of a swarthy young Irishman roaming all over the South Seas.

Flynn's fall from public favor at this time was also a result of the "documentary realism" infiltrating Hollywood movies during the postwar years. The escapist fare at which actors such as Flynn had excelled had flourished during the Depression and World War II because people had wanted to forget the cataclysmic upheavals reshaping the world at that time. Immediately following the war, however, film audiences dwindled, and

BEGINNING OF THE END

those who still went wanted psychological realism and socially conscious movies. Nihilism and despair worked their way into Westerns and crime films, the *film noir* emerged as one of the most powerful forces of personal expression, and consequently there was little room left for the likes of Robin Hood.

Flynn's vehicles from 1945 on were bland exceptions to the prevailing mood settling over postwar Hollywood. In a vain attempt to recapture the successes of *Dodge City* and *Virginia City*, Warner Bros. cast Flynn in *San Antonio*, one of the most pedestrian Westerns ever to come out of the Burbank studios. Except for the elaborate production values, there is little in *San Antonio* to differentiate it from the Monogram and Republic potboilers that filled double bills on Saturday afternoons for years. Characterization and narrative are at a minimum, and, more important, the few action sequences are incredibly flaccid.

Director David Butler stages all of the action set pieces perfunctorily, and the film pokes along for almost an hour and a half, burdened by several musical numbers blandly

SAN ANTONIO (1945). As Clay Hardin

delivered by Alexis Smith and extended low-comedy turns by S.Z. "Cuddles" Sakall (all of which are singularly unfunny). In the final reel of the film, Butler suddenly overplays his hand with a saloon brawl, a stakeout in the Alamo, and an anticlimactic chase across the prairie.

Flynn walks through his role of Clay Hardin, a cattleman who has obtained a black tally book containing proof that Paul Kelly, owner of San Antonio's leading dance hall, is the kingpin of a ruthless rustling syndicate. When the book is stolen by Kelly's Mexican partner (Victor Francen), Flynn's efforts to retrieve it precipitate the principal action of the film. A subplot involving the rivalry and distrust between Kelly and Francen doesn't squeeze much juice into the project.

Flynn's performance is unbelievably *un*physical. He lolls around saloons rolling cigarettes and half-heartedly woos his leading lady (who threatens to evaporate from the screen), but his heart just doesn't seem to be in it. Flynn's often-expressed dislike at doing Westerns is much in evidence in *San Antonio*. He finally works up enough energy to chase Paul Kelly on horseback in the last few minutes of the film, then jumps onto the stagecoach that is carrying Alexis Smith away from San Antonio, and in true Robin Hood style, swings legs first through the window of the stagecoach to rejoin his ladylove. Flynn's eyes are beginning to show signs of the dissipation that will continue to appear with alarming frequency until the end of his career. The descent from the top had begun.

No matter how many fiestas, tamales, and Mexican dances Butler crams into the running time of *San Antonio*, the paucity of characterization and inventive incident consigns it to the very lowest rank of Flynn vehicles. In a sense, *San Antonio* is not even structured around Flynn's persona, so that he finally emerges in the film as the rather ineffectual protagonist of a hopelessly overproduced bore.

Flynn's next film, *Never Say Goodbye* (1946), demonstrates, more than his earlier comedies, a real aptitude for handling light comedy. Unfortunately, the film is one of the most embarrassing vehicles of Flynn's career. James V. Kern directed this charmless "family" comedy about the machinations of a singularly unpleasant little brat to reconcile her estranged parents. The tone of the film is set in the opening scene when a delivery boy asks the little monster (Patti Brady in a precocious imitation of a human being) to sign her "X" for a package. She looks innocently up at him and inquires, "Wouldn't it be better if I signed my own name?" The triple take on the delivery boy's face un-

SAN ANTONIO (1945). With all the cast principals

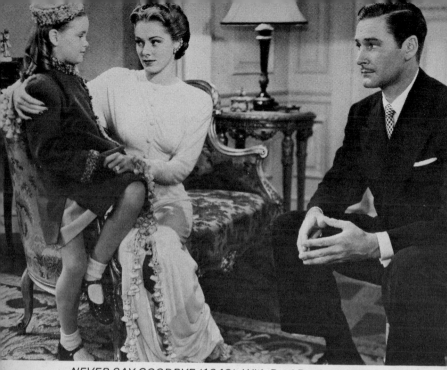

NEVER SAY GOODBYE (1946). With Patti Brady and Eleanor Parker

fortunately sets the tone for the humor that is to follow.

Flynn's scenes with ex-wife Eleanor Parker are as moving as the imbecilic script allows. As the film wobbles to a close, he is forced to undergo a great deal of physical pain in competition for his ex-wife's affection with Forrest Tucker as a returning Marine. The idea of gently needling Flynn's virility has possibilities, but the humor at his expense grows unpleasant and when little Patti Brady nastily tells her father that "Nobody would ever believe you were a tough guy," Flynn looks so forlorn and lost, that one's first impulse is to slap the offensive little darling across the room.

Flynn's first film in 1947, *Cry Wolf*, is yet another depressing manifestation of the actor's declining status with the Warners' executives. Combining the elements of Gothic romance and psychosexual undertones endemic to many forties melodramas, *Cry Wolf's* rather muddled scenario mixes missing wills, hereditary insanity, a formidable Victorian mansion, and other accoutrements of "the old dark house" genre in a most unsatisfying brew. Flynn's role is ambivalently written, and he performs throughout in a disinterested and stilted manner. Casting him in such a role undercuts those aspects of his persona which gave him his appeal; this is the kind of role George Brent could have played in his sleep, and often did.

Flynn is Uncle Mark, guardian to the estate of his mentally unbalanced niece (Geraldine Brooks) and nephew (Richard Basehart). As the film opens, Basehart has just committed suicide and his widow (Barbara Stanwyck) is arriving to claim her share of his inheritance. Matters are complicated by the family's ignorance that Basehart had even been married, so the stage is set for weird noises in the night, secluded laboratories in the "closed wing" of

CRY WOLF (1947). With Barbara Stanwyck

the mansion, and much running down corridors and scrambling over rooftops (most of which is done by Stanwyck, in one of the most physically demanding parts of her career).

Both Flynn and Stanwyck appear to be attempting to stifle laughter during their scenes together. The usually vibrant Stanwyck is even somewhat listless here. The characters are unclearly delineated, and their motivations are inconsistent throughout. Under Peter Godfrey's haphazard direction, *Cry Wolf* emerges as one of the more turgid undertakings of Flynn's career.

Peter Godfrey was at the helm on Flynn's second vehicle in 1947, *Escape Me Never*. This romantic pastiche was based on a story by Margaret Kennedy, author of *The Constant Nymph*, one of the studio's biggest successes of 1943, and a film in which Flynn had originally been set to play the lead opposite Joan Fontaine. (The role eventually went to Charles Boyer.)

Flynn should have stayed out of *Escape Me Never* as well. The film begins promisingly in turn-of-the-century Venice with gondolas, pigeons, and lovely ladies in large hats, beautiful gowns, and parasols, but it soon degenerates into coy whimsy and precious humor. Max Ophuls might have been able to give some visual style to this material, but under Godfrey's direction,

Escape Me Never is lifeless, humorless, and charmless.

Flynn looks as though he's hung over in every scene, and only Ida Lupino manages to transcend her material with a performance of luminous intensity. The moment when she discovers her baby has died of influenza is so extraordinary that it looks as though it were lifted from another movie.

The unlikely casting of Flynn as a struggling composer of classical music and the forced Mitteleuropa quaintness of the *mise-en-scene* combine to make the film seem far longer than its 104-minute running time.

Flynn's next film, *Silver River* (1948), features the best performance of the actor's career, and is the ultimate development of his persona under Raoul Walsh's sympathetic direction. Mike McComb is the closest the actor ever came to playing an anti-hero, and the role itself has the neurotic underpinnings common to many postwar protagonists.

The film opens with Flynn in a familiar act of rebellion against authority. Left in charge of a Union payroll, and ordered not to move from his position, he and his men are attacked by a band of Confederates. He leaves his post and burns the money to prevent the Confederates from getting it.

Cashiered from the service for his

actions, Flynn becomes a gambler, along with sidekick Tom D'Andrea. Flynn manages to parlay his unscrupulous gambling skill into the silver mining game through a series of devious manipulations.

In a poker game, he wins some wagons that are carrying tools and equipment for silver mining to Silver City. He opens a magnificent gambling saloon in Silver City, offers to sell the wagons back to their original owner (Bruce Bennett), and when Bennett offers him shares in his mine instead, Flynn agrees to purchase six thousand shares.

Flynn then has the audacity to court Bennett's headstrong wife, Ann Sheridan. He buys a third interest in Bennett's mine, ties up all the loose cash in town, and proceeds to set up a bank, guaranteeing a weekly payroll for the miners in exchange for a cut in every mine in town.

Flynn's skills as an entrepreneur

ESCAPE ME NEVER (1947). With Ida Lupino

SILVER RIVER (1948). With Ann Sheridan

accelerate his rise as one of the most powerful tyrants on the frontier, but his ruthlessness causes the bankruptcy of the town, the loss of Bennett's life, the loss of his lawyer's friendship, and nearly the end of his relationship with Sheridan.

Silver River is a fascinating study of a megalomaniac. Flynn's Mike McComb is driven by some mysterious inner demon to acquire wealth at the expense of others. He caters to no one but himself, and in the process, almost destroys the one thing that means the most to him, his obsessive love for Sheridan. The key to the film lies in Flynn's relationship with his Shakespeare-quoting, alcoholic lawyer, beautifully played by Thomas Mitchell. Early in the film, Mitchell tells Flynn, "You sound like a lonely man." Flynn replies, "A man is lonely only if he allows himself to be." Mitchell then asks, "What are you looking for?"

Flynn's whole problem in the film is that he really *doesn't* know what he's looking for. He keeps on accumulating wealth and power just for the hell of it. This is the darkest side of the adventurer image, and it is not until the near-tragic conclu-

SILVER RIVER (1948). With Thomas Mitchell, Tom D'Andrea, and Bruce Bennett

On the set of SILVER RIVER (1948) with director Raoul Walsh

sion of the film that Flynn is able to realize Mitchell's lasting hope, that he would channel his very real abilities for leadership into positive, constructive areas of action.

Silver River gave Flynn his most complex and demanding role, and the actor rose to meet the occasion. Flynn was fortunate to have Ann Sheridan as his co-star, as she proved to be the best match for him since Olivia de Havilland. Their fluctuating relationship in the film is delicately conveyed in their many scenes together, and the two achieve an extraordinary rapport in their playing.

Flynn's vulnerability has never been more movingly expressed than the scenes near the end of the film, when Sheridan has left the elaborate mansion he had built especially for her. In one scene, D'Andrea comes to visit, and Flynn is reading a newspaper, standing with his back to the camera, as every item in his house is being re-possessed because of bankruptcy. The mere posture of Flynn's back expresses the loss and despair that have drained this man's body, and when we see his face, there are tears in his eyes. The scene ends with a pan from his forlorn figure to a large portrait of Sheridan—the one item in the house he will not allow the creditors to reclaim.

What is especially remarkable about the film is director Walsh's ability to integrate the development of his fascinating characters into the larger epic structure of his narrative, and yet fuse all of these different elements into an organic whole. *Silver River* is one of the great post-war Westerns, yielding unending riches and discoveries on repeated viewings. It is Flynn's finest hour in the movies.

In a hopeful attempt to revitalize Flynn's waning box-office draw, Warners decided to cast the actor in another swashbuckler, confident that a return to the genre in which he had had his greatest commercial triumphs might yield another hit for the studio. It had been a long time since a Flynn film had reaped a profit, and the actor's period of grace was drawing to a close.

The property chosen was *Adventures of Don Juan* (1949), a project that had been announced for Flynn as early as 1945. Raoul Walsh was originally scheduled to direct, but the director had had severe problems with his old friend on the set of *Silver River* and was not overly anxious to work with him again. Flynn's drinking had become a real problem, and his inability to sustain a scene for very long necessitated shooting much footage around him.

Vincent Sherman (*Mr. Skeffington, The Damned Don't Cry*) was chosen to direct, and after countless delays, shooting began. The result-

ADVENTURES OF DON JUAN (1949). With Viveca Lindfors, Jeanne Shepherd, and Jerry Austin

ing film is most entertaining, and while not up to the level of the best of the Curtiz swashbucklers, it is not appreciably inferior to any of them.

Besides having its fair share of real excitement and spectacle, the film boasts extraordinarily beautiful Technicolor photography by Elwood Bredell. Many of the compositions look as though they had come to life from Renaissance paintings. Warm golds, maroons, emeralds, and lavenders explode across the screen, and the textures of the images themselves emanate a sensuous glow.

Adventures of Don Juan also has the good sense to poke fun at itself and the genre of the swashbuckler. Flynn's persona is subtly parodied in the film, and the very idea of casting the notorious actor as Don Juan is something of a conceit in itself.

The tone of the film is established by a prologue that babbles on about an age in which the frontiers of the mind were continually being extended and broadened. We then see the roguish Don Juan scaling the balcony of a beautiful lady, lifting himself, hand over hand, clambering up the vine-covered trellis. Flynn tells the fair damsel that he has loved her since the beginning of time. "But you only met me yesterday," she reminds him. Without batting an eyelash or missing a beat, he replies, "That was when time began."

If Flynn's transformation from an irresponsible hedonist to the conscientious protector of Queen Margaret's throne is less than plausible, this inconsistency of the characterization does not really damage the film seriously. Perhaps his platonic love for the queen would be more credible if a less glacial actress than Viveca Lindfors had been cast in the role. Lindfors does little to indicate the smoldering passion supposedly burning inside her, and Flynn's devotion to her often seems inexplicable.

The various court intrigues provide ample opportunity for action sequences, and Flynn demonstrates once again his dexterity with a sword. The final duel with Robert Douglas, staged on a grand staircase with a monstrous statue at its peak, is elaborately choreographed, and climaxes with Flynn's bravura leap down the stairs onto his opponent.

Max Steiner's score effectively blends Spanish rhythms with his usual sweeping melodies, and director Sherman reveals a fine eye for detail and decor in his recreation of seventeenth-century Spain. The ending of *Adventures of Don Juan* is a return to the lighter vein of the beginning sequences. Flynn leaves Madrid forever to study abroad, permitting his beloved queen to pursue her regal duties. As he is contemplating his ascetic future with his companion, Alan Hale, a coach passes the two men, its passenger being none other than Nora Eddington (Mrs. Errol Flynn at the time). As he abandons Hale to pursue the lovely lady, Flynn quips, "There's a little bit of Don Juan in every man. Since I *am* Don Juan, there must be more of it in me."

Adventures of Don Juan is per-haps the closest fusion onscreen of Flynn's private reputation with his public persona. Unfortunately, the film did only moderate business, convincing Warners irrevocably that Flynn's days as a star were numbered. Production values and budgets were reduced drastically for all of the actor's subsequent vehicles at the studio.

ADVENTURES OF DON JUAN (1949). With Viveca Lindfors

After a guest spot as Doris Day's childhood sweetheart in the all-star *It's a Great Feeling* (1949), Warner Bros. lent Flynn to MGM to appear opposite Greer Garson in *That Forsyte Woman*. Flynn had signed a new contract with Warners in 1947, allowing him to make one outside film per year. Metro's *Reader's Digest* version of the Galsworthy saga was his first assignment under this new arrangement. It was also his first feature film away from his home studio in almost fifteen years.

Flynn was a good choice for Soames Forsyte, Galsworthy's eminent "man of property." The role should have fulfilled Flynn's often-expressed desire to tackle more challenging roles. Flynn's realization of the role, however, sadly confirms that what he did most often in films, he also did the best. His talents as an actor were genuine, but they had also become circumscribed by the narrow range of the roles in which he had been cast during his career. While Soames Forsyte could have been one of Flynn's most interesting performances, he approaches the role through external manifestations of pomposity and petulance, never delving deeply enough into the character.

Neither Flynn's rigid, wooden performance, nor Greer Garson's lofty, pontifical Irene Forsyte are helped much by Compton

FURTHER DECLINE

Bennett's direction. Bennett was a British director who was riding high at the time on the crest of his success with *The Seventh Veil*. Bennett's talents did not transplant to American soil very well, however; his direction of *That Forsyte Woman* is as arch and stuffy as Miss Garson's perpetually raised right eyebrow.

Screenwriters Jan Lustig, Ivan Tors, and James B. Williams recapitulated the events preceding the opening of *The Man of Property*, chronicling Soames Forsyte's courtship of the beautiful Irene, then jumping into the mainstream of the narrative lifted from the book. The film delineates their subsequent marriage, and the intellectual battle of wills that ensues between his determined possessiveness and her free will. *That Forsyte Woman* is an unbearably smug film, petrified in the "good taste" with which Metro usually molded its adaptations of great literature.

Flynn returned to Warner Bros. for the first of three films he was to make in 1950. *Montana* is a mercifully brief Technicolor Western that once again fights the war between sheepherders and cattle barons.

THAT FORSYTE WOMAN (1949). With Greer Garson

Cheaply made and lethargically directed by Ray Enright (*Dames, The Wagons Roll at Night*), the film has Flynn sauntering through his role as a fighting sheepman with a singular lack of enthusiasm. It is one of his most unprepossessing performances in the very least of his Westerns. *

Alexis Smith, blander than ever, is Flynn's co-star once again. At one point during the film, the actor serenades her with "Reckon I'm in

* Ironically, the Australian-born Flynn was cast as an Australian just twice in the fifty-five films he made during his career. The first time was in *Desperate Journey*; the second, *Montana*.

105

Love," an innocuous little ditty by Mack David, Al Hoffman, and Jerry Livingston. Flynn had performed a similar interlude with Smith in the earlier *San Antonio*.

Flynn's second outing in 1950, *Rocky Mountain*, lacks color, but the overall quality of the film is superior to *Montana*. Flynn plays a Confederate officer on assignment in California to round up outlaws in the hope of controlling the West for the Confederacy. (With the actual Civil War being fought two thousand miles away, one could say that Flynn is the head of a kind of Confederate underground.) During the course of the action, Flynn and his entourage rescue Patrice Wymore from Indians, capture a Union patrol headed by her fiancé (Scott Forbes), and eventually sacrifice their lives to the Indians so that she can escape.

Flynn's role in *Rocky Mountain* is certainly in the tradition of his great screen characters. He is a natural leader among men, sympathetic to their needs, demanding in his expectations of them, and capable of inciting them to controlled outbursts of action against a common enemy. The sacrificial element that appears frequently in the actor's roles is also present here.

Unfortunately, director William Keighley fails to shape Flynn's role in any way that would realize the potential of the character. Flynn himself gives the listless performance that was becoming standard for him around this period. His eyes look more glazed than in any of his previous films.

The two big action sequences in *Rocky Mountain* are staged with some expertise, particularly the final massacre, when Flynn gets a couple of arrows in his back as a result of his chivalrous sacrifice. Keighley, however, fails to make expressive use of some spectacular New Mexico landscapes, except for one suspiciously phallic rock formation which he somehow manages to insert into every long shot.

During the filming of *Rocky Mountain*, Flynn fell in love with his co-star, Patrice Wymore. They were married in Monte Carlo in October 1950.

Flynn was scheduled next to star in *King Solomon's Mines*, again on loan-out to MGM. The actor decided at the last minute, however, that he would rather go on location to India for *Kim*, and the role in the jungle epic went to Stewart Granger. It is interesting in retrospect to speculate on what the lead in *King Solomon's Mines*, one of MGM's biggest grossers of the decade, would have done to recharge Flynn's slumping career.

Kim was one of those properties that had been gathering dust on Metro's shelves for years. First announced as a vehicle for Freddie

THAT FORSYTE WOMAN (1949). With Greer Garson

MONTANA (1950). With Alexis Smith

Bartholomew and Robert Taylor in the late thirties, the project was reactivated in 1942 as a possibility for Mickey Rooney, Conrad Veidt, and Basil Rathbone. When the Office of War Information relayed to Metro its fears that India might be upset by the theme of white supremacy and imperialism implicit in the narrative, the studio abandoned the property until 1950. The new Indian government created in 1948 gave its approval to the screenplay by Leon Gordon, Helen Deutsch, and Richard Schayer, and production began.

Kim is a young orphan, the son of an Irish sergeant, who disguises himself as an Indian in order to survive in his foreign surroundings. During the course of his adventures, he meets a venerable lama (Paul Lukas), an Afghan horse thief doubling as a British government agent (Flynn), and becomes caught up in an intrigue involving Czarist

ROCKY MOUNTAIN (1950). With Chubby Johnson and Patrice Wymore

With wife Patrice Wymore in 1951

Russians who are infiltrating the Khyber Pass.

Unfortunately, Flynn fares no better at the hands of Rudyard Kipling than he did with John Galsworthy. He looks great in his brazen red beard and moustache, his closely cropped sandy hair, his white turban, and his gaudy costumes, but he seldom convinces in what is virtually a supporting role. The actor's relationship with young Kim faintly echoes his relationship with the disguised prince in *The Prince and the Pauper*. In both films Flynn displayed real rapport with his young co-stars, and indeed, it is in his scenes with Dean Stockwell that Flynn comes most alive. The film, in fact, belongs to Stockwell, who gives an engaging performance as Kipling's young hero. His scenes with Paul Lukas' Buddhist priest are the best in the film.

Although *Kim* is lavishly mounted with the traditional opulence of MGM, Victor Saville's stilted direction never really brings the tale to life. Too much footage is given over to endless elephants, caravans, bazaars, and parading British regiments. *Kim's* primary asset is its lush, romantic backgrounds, most of which were filmed on location.

On the way back from shooting *Kim* in India, Flynn made an unfortunate stopover in Italy to appear in a one-hour oddity entitled *Hello,*

God. An old friend of his, William Marshall, produced, wrote, and directed this pacifist fable about an "unknown soldier" who relates a story of four young infantrymen killed on Anzio Beach during World War II.

Flynn's decision to appear in *Hello, God* might have resulted from his intense desire to break his Warners' contract. The studio had specified that his outside films must be "quality" productions. Flynn's appearance in this film is just one of his many self-destructive actions in the last decade of his life.

Having made the film, however, Flynn began to have second thoughts about it. He attempted to block its release, which resulted in all sorts of legal suits and cross-complaints. The upshot of all the turmoil was a shattered relationship between Marshall and Flynn. *Hello, God* was never shown in this country.

While the dissension concerning *Hello, God* was at its peak, Flynn was making another movie under Marshall's direction. Based on an original screenplay by the actor, it was called *Adventures of Captain Fabian* (1951). Mere words can not describe the aesthetic poverty of this Republic potboiler. It is without a doubt the nadir of Flynn's career.

Vestiges of the old Flynn image remain in *Captain Fabian*, although

KIM (1950). As Mahbub Ali, the Red Beard

hey are short-circuited somewhat y the actor's dissipated appearance. His first entrance in the film ccurs while he is taking a bath in a wooden tub aboard his ship. When e goes ashore, he indeed looks the elegant dandy, complete with top at, cutaway coat, and cane. True to orm, all the ladies seem glad to see his faded soldier-of-fortune.

Screenwriter Flynn may have cast himself as a sophisticated, sea-going adventurer, but the actor's appearance gives the lie to such fanciful thinking. Flynn has never looked worse, nor has he ever given a more mechanical performance. Actually, he is barely in the film, disappearing during the middle portions while Micheline Prelle

KIM (1950). With Dean Stockwell

(Presle in her French films), Vincent Price, and Agnes Moorehead fall all over one another with their shameless histrionics.

If *Beam Ends* and *Showdown* weren't proof enough of Flynn's rather limited ability as a writer, the scenario of *Captain Fabian* certainly is. Flynn plays a sea captain who befriends a servant girl (Prelle), wrongly accused of a murder actually committed by the epicene Price. Flynn gets her freed from the charges, and then proceeds to set her up as the proprietress of a waterfront saloon. Both Flynn and Prelle then plot their respective courses of revenge against Price's affluent family. (Flynn's father had been driven to bankruptcy and death by Price's father.)

Flynn was involved in yet another legal tangle over the writing credit for *Captain Fabian*. Another old friend, Charles Gross, filed a suit against the actor in November 1951, claiming that he had done the major work on the adaptation from the novel, *Fabulous Ann Madlock*, on which the film was based.

Flynn's mere appearance as the star of a Republic programmer is a sad indication of the decline his

ADVENTURES OF CAPTAIN FABIAN (1951). With Micheline Prelle

ADVENTURES OF CAPTAIN FABIAN (1951). With Agnes Moorehead

MARA MARU (1952). With Ruth Roman

career was undergoing. His physical countenance continued to de-
teriorate onscreen. *Mara Maru*
(1952) reveals an alarmingly dissipated Flynn. The eyes are dead, the
body is that of a man twice his age,
and the devil-may-care attitude toward life has vanished completely.
Flynn looks drearily depressed by
the ersatz adventure film for which
he returned to Warner Bros. The

studio was now skimping on the
production values in Flynn's films,
especially in the light of their increasingly dubious box-office pros-
pects.

Set in postwar Manila and strik-
ingly photographed in black-and-
white by Robert Burks, *Mara Maru*
casts Flynn as a deep sea diver in
the salvage business, caught up in
the search for a cross of diamonds

buried in a sunken PT boat at the bottom of the ocean. The machinations involving Flynn's partner, the partner's wife (Flynn's former flame), and various other interested parties provide the flimsy base for a picture that never really catches fire.

The first half of the film bogs down in philosophical confrontations about greed and power, but once veteran director Gordon Douglas gets everyone out to sea, things begin to pick up a bit. Flynn's dive for the treasure, the subsequent chase through the jungle, and a final shoot-out in the catacombs of the mission are handled with some flair. If Flynn's conversion at the end of the film seems a bit strained, his performance as a whole is not one of his better ones. Too often he seems embarrassed by the mechanical script and direction, the lack of first-rate production values, and his wooden leading lady, Ruth Roman. She and Flynn ignite few sparks together, and the only characters of real interest in *Mara Maru* are the oily villains portrayed by Raymond Burr and Paul Picerni.

The first shot of Flynn in *Mara Maru* shows him through the mask of his deep sea diving outfit, an apt metaphor for the somewhat restricted performance he gives throughout the course of the film. Attempts are made to revitalize the "dashing lover" image Flynn had projected for so many years (when he enters a local dive, a prostitute stops him with an overeager "Hi, I haven't seen you lately"), but the magic and the charm have all but disappeared. There is an air of resignation in Flynn's performance that would increase as the Fifties continued.

Following the example of many stars during the fifties, Flynn accepted a percentage of the profits, in addition to his salary, for his next picture, *Against All Flags* (1952), made for Universal International. Flynn's swashbuckling corsair was pitted against fiery Maureen O'Hara, the Queen of Technicolor, as a lady pirate with the unlikely name of Spitfire Stevens.

Laid in the eighteenth century, *Against All Flags* finds Flynn, a British naval officer, posing as a deserter in order to infiltrate the Madagascar enclave of pirates led by O'Hara and Anthony Quinn. Flynn aligns himself with the cutthroats and participates in a raid with them on a ship bearing the Emperor of India's daughter (Alice Kelley). Flynn manages to conceal the lady's identity and thus save her life. Having sabotaged the pirates' ammunition in Madagascar, and signaled the British invasion, Flynn sails into the Technicolor sunset with a reformed and domesticated O'Hara.

Flynn reprised a bit of derring-do

in *Against All Flags* that Douglas Fairbanks had introduced in *The Black Pirate* in 1926. In the film's rapier-and-pikestaff finale, the actor (or, more likely, his double), plunges his sword into the ship's sail and rides it as it descends, slitting the white cloth from top to bottom.

Two shorts featuring Flynn in various stages of relaxation and pleasure away from the cameras were also released in 1952. *Cruise of the Zaca* concerned a cruise down the coast of Mexico to the South Seas that Flynn had made in 1946 with his father, his wife Nora, and several friends. The other short, *Deep Sea Fishing*, was a 16mm Kodachrome quickie depicting Flynn and his close friend, archer Howard Hill, fishing for marlin and sailfish near Acapulco. Hill had coached Flynn for the archery sequences in *Robin Hood*, and the two men had remained good friends, fellow hunters and fishermen.

The last film that Flynn made under his Warners' contract, *The Master of Ballantrae* (1953), is one of the more enjoyable, better made Flynn vehicles of the fifties. Flynn himself doesn't bring much to the film, but Jack Cardiff's picturesque

MARA MARU (1952). With Raymond Burr

AGAINST ALL FLAGS (1952). As Brian Hawke

cinematography and an excellent supporting cast of British actors give the film a tone and class lacking in most of Flynn's films around this period. Based on Robert Louis Stevenson's novel, *The Master of Ballantrae* relishes its narrative, and is directed with high style and good spirits by veteran William Keighley.

Flynn's rebel persona remains intact as he goes into exile after fighting in vain for the Stuart cause in the British insurrection of 1745. The principal dramatic conflict arises from Flynn's belief that his brother (Anthony Steel), who remained loyal to King George II, had attempted to murder him to acquire his title of "master of Ballantrae" and marry his fiancée (Beatrice Campbell). The film is almost a glossary of ingredients and incidents from other, more successful Flynn swashbucklers. His uneasy alliance with a French pirate, their orgiastic banquet on Tortuga Bay, and their inevitable duel to the death, evoke *Captain Blood*. At one point Flynn echoes Henry Daniell's statement to him in *The Sea Hawk*, when he refers to himself as having "more lives than a cat."

Flynn moves through the film

THE MASTER OF BALLANTRAE (1953). As Jamie Durisdeer

with more élan than usual at this time, but there is little here to compare with the best of his swashbuckling performances. The energy that was a dominant force in his best roles is gone, never to return. He doesn't even seem terribly interested in all the women who thrust themselves at him. Keighley's lively direction, the sense of adventure and excitement implicit in Stevenson's narrative, and unusually intelligent performances by Roger Livesey, Beatrice Campbell, and Yvonne Furneaux contribute more to the enjoyment of *The Master of Ballantrae* than Flynn's rather world-weary presence.

The most notable aspect of the film is Cardiff's ravishing photography. Misty coasts of Scotland bathed in blue, the white sails of a pirate ship emblazoned against a background of blue sky and sea, and the motley-colored pageantry of the festive ball which greets the prodigal Flynn upon his unexpected return to Scotland, all are filtered through Cardiff's camera with a crispness and clarity that give the film the charm of a beautifully illustrated storybook.

Flynn's sole 1954 feature,

CROSSED SWORDS (1954). With Gina Lollobrigida

Crossed Swords, was a lame follow-up to *Adventures of Don Juan*. Co-produced with friend Barry Mahon and a group of Italian filmmakers, this pallid imitation of a swashbuckler boasted the beautiful Gina Lollobrigida as Flynn's co-star, and again, Jack Cardiff's exquisite color photography. Flynn had never looked more disinterested, and the movie was barely noticed. It did, however, spur the same group into a second venture, an elaborate mounting of *William Tell*, to be shot in CinemaScope by Jack Cardiff, who was to make his directorial debut as well.

After Flynn had put up half the budget for the project, filming began in Italy in the early summer of 1953. Approximately thirty minutes of the film had been shot when the Italians informed Flynn that there was no more money. Lawsuits erupted all over the place. After a great deal of thrashing about in and out of court, the hubbub gradually subsided, leaving in its wake a practically destitute Flynn.

Flynn's experience with the abortive *William Tell* project was not the only worry the actor had in 1953. The United States government slapped him with $1,000,000 in back taxes. After disposing of most of his property and attempting to work off his debts, the actor escaped to the *Zaca*, where he lived on and off for the next four years.

Herbert Wilcox, the prolific producer-director of musical valentines to his wife Anna Neagle, rescued Flynn by casting him in a 1955 film, *Let's Make Up* (British title: *Lilacs in the Spring*). Wilcox's fortuitous intervention went a long way toward salvaging Flynn, spiritually as well as financially.

Unfortunately, neither of the films the actor starred in opposite Miss Neagle, a charming lady of questionable talent, did much to revive his career. *Let's Make Up* is a period backstage musical in which Miss Neagle portrays a World War II entertainer who blacks out during an air raid, and then proceeds to imagine herself as Nell Gwyn, Queen Victoria, and her own mother.

Flynn is fairly charming as Miss Neagle's *vis-à-vis*, and the film provides him with the opportunity to perform an engaging soft-shoe number with his co-star.

The English box-office success of *Let's Make Up* prompted a second pairing of this unlikely duo. Ivor Novello's light opera, *King's Rhapsody*, was taken out of mothballs, spruced up a bit (but not enough), and turned into an opulent CinemaScope musical romance. Ironically, most of the singing and dancing in the film was done by Patrice Wymore, Anna Neagle's musical numbers having been excised from the final release print.

WILLIAM TELL (incomplete, 1953). With Franco Interlenghi

LET'S MAKE UP (1955). With Anna Neagle

Though lovely to look at, *King's Rhapsody* (1955) is even more turgid than its predecessor. Neither film reveals Wilcox as a major threat to Vincente Minnelli, Stanley Donen or even George Sidney.

Flynn managed to sandwich *The Warriors* (1955) in between the two films he made with Miss Neagle. His last swashbuckler, *The Warriors* has little to recommend it. It is a sad farewell to the genre in which Flynn was peerless for almost two decades.

KING'S RHAPSODY (1955). With Anna Neagle

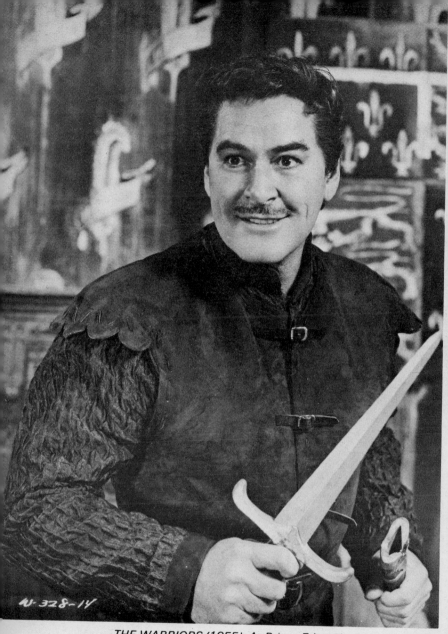

THE WARRIORS (1955). As Prince Edward

N·328-14

ISTANBUL (1956). With Cornell Borchers

The actor was cast as Prince Edward of England, better known in legend and folklore as the Black Prince. Ensconced in France to protect land that has been usurped from his father, King Edward III, he spends most of the film in conflict with the French lords who want to rid their country of him. A romantic triangle among Flynn, Joanne Dru, and Peter Finch fails to enliven the proceedings, most of which resemble a tired rehash of *Ivanhoe*. (The same castle was used for key sequences in both films.)

Henry Levin's direction of *The Warriors* is an object lesson in the unimaginative employment of CinemaScope, and Flynn looks far too old to be playing the young prince. In most of his scenes, he looks as though he had just gotten out of bed.

Nineteen fifty-five was one of Flynn's worst years, personally as well as professionally. The most casual observer could predict that his career was drawing to a close. In 1956, however, Flynn's cruises aboard the Zaca were interrupted by an offer to appear opposite Universal-International's latest discovery, Miss Cornell Borchers, in *Istanbul*. Thinking the film would be shot on location in Turkey, Flynn ignored his doubts about the script and director Joseph Pevney, and accepted the role. The opportunity to travel to an unknown country always intrigued Flynn; in fact, it had been the very factor that had prompted him to choose *Kim* over *King Solomon's Mines* in 1950.

Universal's decision to use CinemaScope inserts for *Istanbul* was a severe disappointment to the actor, and he trudges through this unappetizing little melodrama of romance and intrigue with evident distaste for the third-rate production in which he's found himself.

Flynn again plays a soldier-of-fortune in *Istanbul*. On purchasing an Oriental bracelet in which thirteen precious diamonds are embedded he becomes the target of repeated attempts by customs officials and smugglers to retrieve the stones. His innocent participation in this intrigue results in his deportation, but he returns several years later to the hotel room in which he had hidden the gems. The convolutions of the incredibly complicated plot overpower director Pevney; he fails to shape the material in an exciting or interesting manner. The film is a shambles from beginning to end.

Miss Borchers, a German actress with a somewhat matronly beauty, had first appeared in Fox's *The Big Lift* in 1950 and, after five years in Europe, starred in a moderately successful British film, *The Divided Heart*. Universal signed her to a contract, but the programmers in which they cast her failed to reveal any distinctive personality or talent. In *Istanbul* she plays Flynn's wife, who contracts amnesia when he is deported, and marries Torin Thatcher during her husband's absence.

Istanbul was a remake of *Singapore*, filmed in 1947 with Fred MacMurray and Ava Gardner. Bosley Crowther commented in his review of the film in *The New York Times* that Flynn was "looking heavily enameled about the eyes and jaws."

Concurrently with the release of *Istanbul* in 1956, Flynn embarked upon the production of a syndicated television series in England. Called *The Errol Flynn Theatre*, the actor himself introduced each segment and acted in six of them. The show lasted only one season.

By 1957 it was clear to most people that Errol Flynn was washed up, a has-been. After many years as

ISTANBUL (1956). As Jim Brennan

a top-ranking star and the epitome of the dashing screen hero, he had become something of a running joke to the Hollywood wags who revel in the professional and personal decline of movie stars.

The years of narcotics, excessive drinking, and sensual indulgence had begun to consume Errol Flynn. He was now forty-eight, and he looked sixty-eight. The magnificent looks that had forged his career had deteriorated. The charm still filtered through occasionally, but the old vitality had disappeared forever.

Flynn looked enervated in his first 1957 effort, a low-budget exercise titled *The Big Boodle*. Flynn again accepted the role primarily because the film was shot almost entirely in Havana, Cuba. He had become interested in the imminent upheavals mounting in Cuba, aligning himself with the rebels' cause much as he had done twenty years earlier when he thrust himself into the heart of the Spanish Civil War.

Modestly directed by Richard Wilson, who assisted Orson Welles on his aborted *It's All True* project and also directed such respectable crime films as *Al Capone* and *Pay Or Die*, *The Big Boodle* makes fairly expressive use of its locations, which include the streets and plazas of Havana, various seedy night clubs and gambling holes, and diverse historical monuments. The Morro Castle provides the setting for the lengthy gun battle that climaxes the picture.

Flynn, looking jowly and weary, plays a croupier in a gambling den who becomes involved in a counterfeit plot when a blonde temptress (Rossana Rory) slips him a bogus bill at the gambling table. The film becomes a double chase, as the authorities and crooks go after Flynn, thinking he knows where the bogus plates are hidden, and Flynn himself decides to pursue the crooks.

The plot and Flynn's role bear striking similarities to *Istanbul*, but this time the actor has both Miss Rory and Gia Scala battling over his faded charms.

Just when Flynn thought he would never escape grinding out these third-rate melodramas, Darryl F. Zanuck stepped into the picture. Zanuck felt that Flynn would be ideal casting for the role of Mike Campbell in his upcoming film version of Ernest Hemingway's *The Sun Also Rises* (1957). Reportedly, Flynn was hesitant to accept the role, inasmuch as the part was radically different from any other in his career; but at the insistence of Zanuck, and with the encouragement of Patrice Wymore, Flynn relented. It must have also been difficult for Flynn to accept fourth billing, since he had received top, or co-starring, billing for twenty-two years.

THE BIG BOODLE (1957). With Rossana Rory

BB-(113)-66

Viewing the film today, one wonders at Flynn's reluctance. As conceived by director Henry King, the character Flynn plays does not have an ounce of the emotional resonance of depth of feeling Flynn brought to such roles as George Custer, James Corbett, or Mike McComb. Indeed, Flynn seems closer to merely playing himself here than he ever did under Curtiz and Walsh, in whose films contemporary critics often accused him of merely projecting his private self onto a public persona.

Mike Campbell is a bankrupt sot, an empty shell of a man who is repeatedly abandoned and humiliated by the wanton Lady Brett Ashley (Ava Gardner in a remarkably passive performance). Flynn *looks* right in the role; his characterization is greatly abetted by the beret, cigarette holder, binoculars, and canteen King has given him to flesh out his performance. The knowledge of Flynn's personal decay hinders the viewer from total belief in the performance, however; when he flashes the wan reflection of that once-dazzling smile, and says, "Nobody seems to pay much attention

THE SUN ALSO RISES (1957). With Tyrone Power

THE SUN ALSO RISES (1957). With Ava Gardner

to me anymore," the aesthetic distance between role and actor disappears.

Certainly Flynn's role, and the personal reverberations he brings to it, are the most interesting aspects of this inflated bore of a movie. *The Sun Also Rises* is suffused with the perfunctory pictorialism that marks all of director King's adaptations of "literary masterpieces," such as *Tender Is the Night* and *The Snows of Kilimanjaro*. Zanuck inexplicably felt that the presence of Tyrone Power in his "prestige" productions had some ennobling effect on the project (*viz., The Razor's Edge*), and his casting of this lifeless actor as the impotent Jake Barnes is hilariously appropriate. Power is so bland that he evaporates from the screen before one's eyes. The casting of Power is surpassed only by Mel Ferrer as a boxer. *The Sun Also Rises* sets before the Fox logo disappears from the screen.

Flynn got good notices, however, and the "comeback" engendered by his personal success in the film briefly recharged his career. Jack L. Warner confesses in his autobiography that he never considered anyone but Flynn for the role of John Barrymore in *Too Much, Too Soon* (1958), the film that was to bring the actor back to Warner Bros. for the first time in five years.

Warner adds, however, that Flynn was drunk during most of the shooting.

Maybe Flynn was watching the rushes. *Too Much, Too Soon* is so bad it's funny. Adapted by Art and Jo Napoleon from Diana Barrymore's self-pitying autobiography, this film has to be seen to be believed.

Flynn apparently was anxious to play the role. John Barrymore had been one of his closest friends, and the two actors' lives shared certain obvious parallels. Perhaps Flynn was too close to the part, or perhaps he was too far gone during the filming, but for whatever reason, his performance is a failure. He does have his moments in the film, but the total absence of astute direction renders his characterization chaotic and incoherent. At times Flynn seems to be burlesquing not only Barrymore, but himself as well.

Depressing as it is, Flynn's appearance in this tawdry little tale is the brightest spot in the movie. When he dies midway through the film, *Too Much, Too Soon* degenerates even further into a sordid parade of paramours, sadists, and occasional husbands mistreating and abusing a perpetually sneering Dorothy Malone. Her misguided performance as Diana Barrymore conspires with the screenplay's sophomoric dialogue to produce

TOO MUCH, TOO SOON (1958). With Dorothy Malone

most of the unintentional humor in the film.

Early in 1958, Flynn returned to the stage in *The Master of Thornfield*, Huntington Hartford's adaptation of Charlotte Brontë's *Jane Eyre*. Flynn was totally incapable of sustaining a live performance by this time (he couldn't even memorize the lines), and after dis-mal tryouts in Detroit and Cincinnati, Hartford wisely closed the play.

Again, Darryl F. Zanuck came to the rescue by casting Flynn in the film version of Romain Gary's novel, *The Roots of Heaven* (1958). Although Flynn receives top billing in the movie, his footage with dialogue laid end to end couldn't be

TOO MUCH, TOO SOON (1958). With Dorothy Malone

THE ROOTS OF HEAVEN (1958). With Juliette Greco

THE ROOTS OF HEAVEN (1958). With Juliette Greco

more than fifteen minutes. He hovers in the background through much of the later portions of the film, but his contribution is minimal. It is immensely distressing to see Flynn in a state of emotional and physical breakdown toward the end of his career and life. One year after *The Roots of Heaven*, he was dead. The furor over Flynn's "comeback" in the late fifties assumes, in retrospect, the aspect of public curiosity in a particularly unpleasant form of public dissipation. That Zanuck was so eager to cast Flynn in parts so uncomfortably close to his real existence smacks of the cruelest, most sensational exploitation. Flynn's hands tremble, his eyes water, and the discomfort he, as an actor, is so obviously experiencing is painfully, embarrassingly transmitted to the viewer.

Flynn's relation to the central conflict of the film is peripheral. The narrative centers around Morel (Trevor Howard), a fanatic who is dedicated to the preservation of the elephant. To achieve this end, he repeatedly sabotages ivory hunters and refineries. Morel envisions the elephant as the very image of free-

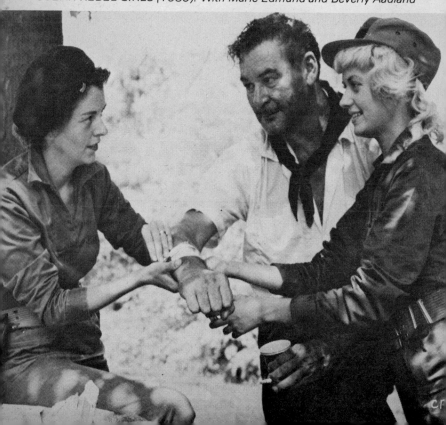

CUBAN REBEL GIRLS (1959). With Marie Edmund and Beverly Aadland

dom and space that enabled him to survive a German POW camp. When Morel's acts against the ivory industry force him into exile, a woman of easy virtue (Juliette Greco) and a sot who had informed on fellow officers to the Nazis (Flynn) follow Morel to the elephants' watering hole and grazing fields. The film disintegrates into a series of absurd jibes at the media (Orson Welles as a TV entrepreneur and Eddie Albert as a magazine photographer who undergoes a totally irrational metamorphosis at the film's end), and pretentious philosophizing on ecology, freedom, friendship, and dignity, not necessarily in that order.

The symbolism of this didactic allegory is as thick as the skin of the pachyderm about which it is ostensibly so concerned. Director John Huston and Romain Gary, who coadapted his novel with Patrick Leigh-Fermor for the screen, have done little more than film a tract —one that does not even have the courage of its convictions. Its concerns are verbalized too often. Each character spouts self-aware philosophy every five minutes. We learn about the characters only through what the other characters say about them. It's the kind of film in which a bald German aristocrat with a monocle speaks fourteen languages but remains mute, communicating only through guttural grunts, because of the injustice and inequity of the world.

For all the hoopla surrounding the location shooting in French Equatorial Africa, a venture that induced sunstroke, malaria, and dysentery among members of the company, Huston's use of exterior footage is, as usual, perfunctory and uninspired. Huston's heavy, pretentious style and Gary's allegorical aspirations conspire to produce an elephantine bore.

Flynn found himself out of favor once again after the critical and commercial disaster of *The Roots of Heaven*. His next and last film, *Cuban Rebel Girls* (1959), was a semidocumentary filmed in Cuba. It featured fifteen-year-old Beverly Aadland, who was the actor's constant companion during the last months of his life.

Cuban Rebel Girls is an incredibly squalid little item. Directed by Barry Mahon, Flynn's old friend from the *Crossed Swords-William Tell* days, and written and narrated by Flynn himself, the film is an unappetizing potpourri of dubbed dialogue, newsreel clips, static action sequences, and amateurishly acted confrontations. Flynn wrote himself into the proceedings as "a correspondent for the Hearst press." The nubile Miss Aadland portrays an American girl in love

with a mercenary who is aiding the insurgents.

Cuban Rebel Girls may be a depressing ending to Flynn's film career, but it was not his actual last acting role. Under Arthur Hiller's direction, he played a peddler roaming the Wild West in a thirty-minute television segment, *The Golden Shanty*. Hiller has reported since that the actor's memory was so fuzzy that giant teleprompters were installed all over the set, so that Flynn could read his lines from any position.

Flynn's last professional appearance was on Red Skelton's television show in October, 1959. A week later, he was dead. The doctors in Vancouver, B.C., where he had gone to sell his beloved *Zaca*, attributed his death to a heart attack. Flynn's liver and kidneys had been eaten away over the years by alcohol, drugs, and his recurring bouts with malaria, tuberculosis, gonorrhea, and acute hepatitis. He was buried on October 20, 1959, in Forest Lawn Cemetery.

Flynn's autobiography, *My Wicked, Wicked Ways*, published in the year of his death, is an innocuous memoir, revealing little self-awareness on his part. Flynn the man will probably always remain an enigma, which is as it should be. Familiarity with a star's personal life inevitably detracts from the legend.

Flynn had a glorious career, despite its rapid disintegration during the last decade of his life. Leaping from tree to tree in Sherwood Forest, leading his doomed troops in battle against a horde of Indians, battling in the boxing ring against John L. Sullivan, he embodied the screen hero too brave, too foolhardy, to consider the consequences of his actions. The bold vigor and gallant chivalry, laced with wry impudence, that characterized his most colorful performances is his testament to succeeding generations of moviegoers. What a drab world it would be if there had never been an Errol Flynn!

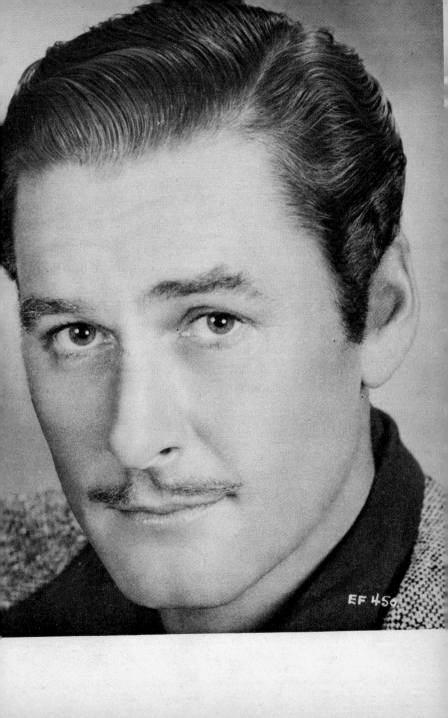

EF 450

BIBLIOGRAPHY

Behlmer, Rudy. *Memo from David O. Selznick*. New York: The Viking Press, 1972.

Flynn, Errol. *My Wicked, Wicked Ways*. New York: G.P. Putnam's Sons, 1959.

Goodman, Ezra. *The Fifty-Year Decline and Fall of Hollywood*. New York: MacFadden-Bartell Corp., 1961.

New York Times Film Reviews, The: 1913-1968, Vols. 4, 5. New York: The New York Times and Arno Press, 1970.

Sarris, Andrew. *The American Cinema*. New York: E.P. Dutton, 1968.

Schickel, Richard. *The Stars*. New York: The Dial Press, 1962.

Sennett, Ted. *Warner Brothers Presents*. New Rochelle: Arlington House, 1971.

Shipman, David. *The Great Movie Stars: The Golden Years*. New York: Crown, 1970.

Thomas, Tony, Behlmer, Rudy and McCarty, Clifford. *The Films of Errol Flynn*. Secaucus: The Citadel Press, 1969.

Warner, Jack L. *My First Hundred Years in Hollywood*. New York: Random House, 1964.

THE FILMS OF ERROL FLYNN

The director's name follows the release date. A (c) following the release date indicates that the film is in color. Sp indicates Screenplay and b/o indicates based/on.

1. IN THE WAKE OF THE BOUNTY. Expeditionary Films, 1933. *Charles Chauvel.* Sp: Charles Chauvel. Cast: Mayne Lynton, Victor Gourier, John Warwick, Patricia Penman.

2. MURDER AT MONTE CARLO. Warner Bros., 1935. *Ralph Ince.* Sp: Michael Barringer, b/o story by Tom Van Dycke. Cast: Eve Gray, Paul Graetz, Lawrence Hanray, Ellis Irving, Henry Victor.

3. THE CASE OF THE CURIOUS BRIDE. Warner Bros., 1935. *Michael Curtiz.* Sp: Tom Reed, b/o novel by Erle Stanley Gardner. Cast: Warren William, Margaret Lindsay, Donald Woods, Claire Dodd, Allen Jenkins, Philip Reed, Barton MacLane, Winifred Shaw.

4. DON'T BET ON BLONDES. Warner Bros., 1935. *Robert Florey.* Sp: Isabel Dawn and Boyce DeGaw. Cast: Warren William, Guy Kibbee, Claire Dodd, William Gargan, Vince Barnett.

5. CAPTAIN BLOOD. Warner Bros., 1935. *Michael Curtiz.* Sp: Casey Robinson, b/o novel by Rafael Sabatini. Cast: Olivia de Havilland, Lionel Atwill, Basil Rathbone, Ross Alexander, Guy Kibbee, Henry Stephenson, Robert Barrat, Hobart Cavanaugh, Donald Meek, Jessie Ralph. Previously filmed in 1923.

6. THE CHARGE OF THE LIGHT BRIGADE. Warner Bros., 1936. *Michael Curtiz.* Sp: Michel Jacoby and Rowland Leigh, b/o story by Michel Jacoby. Cast: Olivia de Havilland, Patric Knowles, Henry Stephenson, Nigel Bruce, Donald Crisp, David Niven.

7. GREEN LIGHT. Warner Bros., 1937. *Frank Borzage.* Sp: Milton Krims, b/o novel by Lloyd C. Douglas. Cast: Anita Louise, Margaret Lindsay, Sir Cedric Hardwicke, Walter Abel, Henry O'Neill.

8. THE PRINCE AND THE PAUPER. Warner Bros., 1937. *William Keighley.* Sp: Laird Doyle, b/o novel by Mark Twain. Cast: Claude Rains, Henry Stephenson, Barton MacLane, Billy Mauch, Bobby Mauch, Alan Hale, Eric Portman, Montagu Love. Previously filmed in 1915 and 1923.

9. ANOTHER DAWN. Warner Bros., 1937. *William Dieterle.* Sp: Laird Doyle. Cast: Kay Francis, Ian Hunter, Frieda Inescourt, Herbert Mundin, G.P. Huntley, Jr.

10. THE PERFECT SPECIMEN. Warner Bros., 1937. *Michael Curtiz.* Sp: Norman Reilly Raine, Lawrence Riley, Brewster Morse, and Fritz Falkenstein, b/o story by Samuel Hopkins Adams. Cast: Joan Blondell, Hugh Herbert, Edward Everett Horton, Dick Foran, Beverly Roberts, May Robson, Allen Jenkins, Dennie Moore.

11. THE ADVENTURES OF ROBIN HOOD. Warner Bros., 1938 (c). *Michael Curtiz and William Keighley.* Sp: Norman Reilly Raine and Seton I. Miller, b/o Robin Hood legends. Cast: Olivia de Havilland, Basil Rathbone, Claude Rains, Patric Knowles, Eugene Pallette, Alan Hale, Melville Cooper, Ian Hunter, Una O'Connor, Herbert Mundin, Montagu Love.

12. FOUR'S A CROWD. Warner Bros., 1938. *Michael Curtiz.* Sp: Casey Robinson and Sig Herzig, b/o story by Wallace Sullivan. Cast: Olivia de Havilland, Rosalind Russell, Patric Knowles, Walter Connolly, Hugh Herbert, Melville Cooper, Franklin Pangborn.

13. THE SISTERS. Warner Bros., 1938. *Anatole Litvak.* Sp: Milton Krims, b/o novel by Myron Brinig. Cast: Bette Davis, Anita Louise, Ian Hunter, Donald Crisp, Beulah Bondi, Jane Bryan, Alan Hale, Dick Foran, Henry Travers, Patric Knowles, Lee Patrick.

13. THE DAWN PATROL. Warner Bros., 1938. *Edmund Goulding.* Sp: Seton I. Miller and Dan Totheroh, b/o story by John Monk Saunders and Howard Hawks. Cast: Basil Rathbone, David Niven, Donald Crisp, Melville Cooper, Barry Fitzgerald, Carl Esmond. Previously filmed in 1930.

15. DODGE CITY. Warner Bros., 1939 (c). *Michael Curtiz.* Sp: Robert Buckner. Cast: Olivia de Havilland, Ann Sheridan, Bruce Cabot, Frank McHugh, Alan Hale, John Litel, Henry Travers, Henry O'Neill, Victor Jory, William Lundigan, Guinn "Big Boy" Williams.

16. THE PRIVATE LIVES OF ELIZABETH AND ESSEX. Warner Bros., 1939 (c). *Michael Curtiz.* Sp: Norman Reilly Raine and Aeneas MacKenzie, b/o play by Maxwell Anderson. Cast: Bette Davis, Olivia de Havilland, Donald Crisp, Alan Hale, Vincent Price, Henry Stephenson, Henry Daniell, James Stephenson, Nanette Fabares (Fabray).

17. VIRGINIA CITY. Warner Bros., 1940. *Michael Curtiz.* Sp: Robert Buckner. Cast: Miriam Hopkins, Randolph Scott, Humphrey Bogart, Frank McHugh,

Alan Hale, Guinn "Big Boy" Williams, John Litel, Douglass Dumbrille, Moroni Olsen.

18. THE SEA HAWK. Warner Bros., 1940. *Michael Curtiz*. Sp: Howard Koch and Seton I. Miller, b/o novel by Rafael Sabatini. Cast: Brenda Marshall, Claude Rains, Donald Crisp, Flora Robson, Alan Hale, Henry Daniell, Una O'Connor, James Stephenson, Gilbert Roland, William Lundigan. Previously filmed in 1924.

19. SANTA FE TRAIL. Warner Bros., 1940. *Michael Curtiz*. Sp: Robert Buckner. Cast: Olivia de Havilland, Raymond Massey, Ronald Reagan, Alan Hale, William Lundigan, Van Heflin, Gene Reynolds, Henry O'Neill, Guinn "Big Boy" Williams, Alan Baxter.

20. FOOTSTEPS IN THE DARK. Warner Bros., 1941. *Lloyd Bacon*. Sp: Lester Cole and John Wexley, b/o play by Laszlo Fodor, Bernard Mervale and Jeffrey Dell. Cast: Brenda Marshall, Ralph Bellamy, Alan Hale, Lee Patrick, Allen Jenkins, Lucile Watson, William Frawley, Roscoe Karns.

21. DIVE BOMBER. Warner Bros., 1941 (c). *Michael Curtiz*. Sp: Frank Wead and Robert Buckner, b/o story by Frank Wead. Cast: Fred MacMurray, Ralph Bellamy, Alexis Smith, Robert Armstrong, Regis Toomey, Allen Jenkins, Craig Stevens, Herbert Anderson, Moroni Olsen, Dennie Moore, Louis Jean Heydt.

22. THEY DIED WITH THEIR BOOTS ON. Warner Bros., 1941. *Raoul Walsh*. Sp: Wally Klein and Aeneas MacKenzie. Cast: Olivia de Havilland, Arthur Kennedy, Charley Grapewin, Gene Lockhart, Anthony Quinn, Stanley Ridges, John Litel, Walter Hampden, Sydney Greenstreet, Regis Toomey, Hattie McDaniel.

23. DESPERATE JOURNEY. Warner Bros., 1942. *Raoul Walsh*. Sp: Arthur T. Horman. Cast: Ronald Reagan, Nancy Coleman, Raymond Massey, Alan Hale, Arthur Kennedy, Ronald Sinclair, Albert Basserman, Sig Rumann.

24. GENTLEMAN JIM. Warner Bros., 1942. *Raoul Walsh*. Sp: Vincent Lawrence and Horace McCoy, b/o James J. Corbett's autobiography. Cast: Alexis Smith, Jack Carson, Alan Hale, John Loder, William Frawley, Minor Watson, Ward Bond, Madeleine LeBeau, Rhys Williams, Arthur Shields, Dorothy Vaughan, James Flavin.

25. EDGE OF DARKNESS. Warner Bros., 1943. *Lewis Milestone*. Sp: Robert Rossen, b/o novel by William Woods. Cast: Ann Sheridan, Walter Huston, Nancy Coleman, Helmut Dantine, Judith Anderson, Ruth Gordon, John Beal, Morris Carnovsky, Charles Dingle.

26. **THANK YOUR LUCKY STARS.** Warner Bros., 1943. *David Butler*. Sp: Norman Panama, Melvin Frank, and James V. Kern, b/o story by Everett Freeman and Arthur Schwartz. Cast: Humphrey Bogart, Eddie Cantor, Bette Davis, Olivia de Havilland, John Garfield, Joan Leslie, Ida Lupino, Dennis Morgan, Ann Sheridan, Dinah Shore, Alexis Smith, Jack Carson, Alan Hale, George Tobias.

27. **NORTHERN PURSUIT.** Warner Bros., 1943. *Raoul Walsh*. Sp: Frank Gruber and Alvah Bessie, b/o story by Leslie T. White. Cast: Julie Bishop, Helmut Dantine, John Ridgely, Gene Lockhart, Tom Tully.

28. **UNCERTAIN GLORY.** Warner Bros., 1944. *Raoul Walsh*. Sp: Laszlo Vadnay and Max Brand, b/o story by Joe May and Laszlo Vadnay. Cast: Paul Lukas, Jean Sullivan, Lucile Watson, Faye Emerson, James Flavin, Douglass Dumbrille, Dennis Hoey, Sheldon Leonard.

29. **OBJECTIVE BURMA.** Warner Bros., 1945. *Raoul Walsh*. Sp: Ranald MacDougall and Lester Cole, b/o story by Alvah Bessie. Cast: James Brown, William Prince, George Tobias, Henry Hull, Warner Anderson, John Alvin, Stephen Richards, Richard Erdman, Anthony Caruso.

30. **SAN ANTONIO.** Warner Bros., 1945 (c). *David Butler*. Sp: Alan LeMay and W.R. Burnett. Cast: Alexis Smith, S.Z. Sakall, Victor Francen, Florence Bates, John Litel, Paul Kelly.

31. **NEVER SAY GOODBYE.** Warner Bros., 1946. *James V. Kern*. Sp: I.A.L. Diamond and James V. Kern, b/o story by Ben and Norma Barzman. Cast: Eleanor Parker, Patti Brady, Lucile Watson, S.Z. Sakall, Forrest Tucker, Donald Woods, Peggy Knudsen, Tom D'Andrea, Hattie McDaniel.

32. **CRY WOLF.** Warner Bros., 1947. *Peter Godfrey*. Sp: Catherine Turney, b/o novel by Marjorie Carleton. Cast: Barbara Stanwyck, Geraldine Brooks, Richard Basehart, Jerome Cowan, John Ridgely.

33. **ESCAPE ME NEVER.** Warner Bros., 1947. *Peter Godfrey*. Sp: Thames Williamson, b/o novel and play by Margaret Kennedy. Cast: Ida Lupino, Eleanor Parker, Gig Young, Reginald Denny, Isobel Elsom. Previously filmed in 1935.

34. **SILVER RIVER.** Warner Bros., 1948. *Raoul Walsh*. Sp: Stephen Longstreet and Harriet Frank, Jr., b/o unpublished novel by Stephen Longstreet. Cast: Ann Sheridan, Thomas Mitchell, Bruce Bennett, Tom D'Andrea, Barton MacLane.

35. **ADVENTURES OF DON JUAN.** Warner Bros., 1949 (c). *Vincent Sherman*.

Sp: George Oppenheimer and Harry Kurnitz, b/o story by Herbert Dalmas. Cast: Viveca Lindfors, Robert Douglas, Alan Hale, Romney Brent, Ann Rutherford, Robert Warwick, Jerry Austin, Douglas Kennedy.

36. IT'S A GREAT FEELING. Warner Bros., 1949 (c). *David Butler*. Sp: Jack Rose and Melville Shavelson, b/o story by I.A.L. Diamond. Cast: Dennis Morgan, Doris Day, Jack Carson, Gary Cooper, Joan Crawford, Sydney Greenstreet, Danny Kaye, Patricia Neal, Eleanor Parker, Ronald Reagan, Edward G. Robinson, Jane Wyman.

37. THAT FORSYTE WOMAN. MGM, 1949 (c). *Compton Bennett*. Sp: Jan Lustig, Ivan Tors, and James B. Williams, b/o novel by John Galsworthy. Cast: Greer Garson, Walter Pidgeon, Robert Young, Janet Leigh, Harry Davenport, Aubrey Mather.

38. MONTANA. Warner Bros., 1950 (c). *Ray Enright*. Sp: James R. Webb, Borden Chase, and Charles O'Neal, b/o story by Ernest Haycox. Cast: Alexis Smith, S:Z. Sakall, Douglas Kennedy, James Brown, Ian MacDonald.

39. ROCKY MOUNTAIN. Warner Bros., 1950. *William Keighley*. Sp: Winston Miller and Alan LeMay, b/o story by Alan LeMay. Cast: Patrice Wymore, Scott Forbes, Guinn "Big Boy" Williams, Dick Jones, Howard Petrie, Slim Pickens, Chubby Johnson, Buzz Henry.

40. KIM. MGM, 1950 (c). *Victor Saville*. Sp: Leon Gordon, Helen Deutsch, and Richard Schayer, b/o novel by Rudyard Kipling. Cast: Dean Stockwell, Paul Lukas, Robert Douglas, Thomas Gomez, Cecil Kellaway, Arnold Moss, Reginald Owen, Laurette Luez.

41. HELLO, GOD. No U.S. release, 1951. *William Marshall*. Sp: William Marshall. Cast: Sherry Jackson, Joe Mazzuca, Armando Formica.

42. THE ADVENTURES OF CAPTAIN FABIAN. Republic, 1951. *William Marshall*. Sp: Errol Flynn, b/o novel by Robert Shannon. Cast: Micheline Prelle (Presle), Vincent Price, Agnes Moorehead, Victor Francen.

43. MARA MARU. Warner Bros., 1952. *Gordon Douglas*. Sp: N. Richard Nash, b/o story by Philip Yordan, Sidney Harmon, and Hollister Noble. Cast: Ruth Roman, Raymond Burr, Paul Picerni, Richard Webb, Dan Seymour.

44. AGAINST ALL FLAGS. Universal, 1952 (c). *George Sherman*. Sp: Aeneas MacKenzie and Joseph Hoffman, b/o story by Aeneas MacKenzie. Cast: Maureen O'Hara, Anthony Quinn, Alice Kelley, Mildred Natwick, Robert Warwick.

45. THE MASTER OF BALLANTRAE. Warner Bros., 1953 (c). *William Keighley*. Sp: Herb Meadow, b/o novel by Robert Louis Stevenson. Cast: Roger

Livesey, Anthony Steel, Beatrice Campbell, Yvonne Furneaux, Felix Aylmer, Mervyn Johns, Charles Goldner.

46. CROSSED SWORDS. A Viva Film, released by United Artists, 1954 (c). *Milton Krims*. Sp: Milton Krims. Cast: Gina Lollobrigida, Cesare Danova, Nadia Gray, Paola Mori, Roldano Lupi.

47. LET'S MAKE UP. An Everest Film, released by United Artists, 1955 (c). *Herbert Wilcox*. Sp: Miles Malleson, b/o play by Harold Purcell. Cast: Anna Neagle, David Farrar, Kathleen Harrison, Peter Graves, Helen Haye.

48. THE WARRIORS. Allied Artists, 1955 (c). *Henry Levin*. Sp: Daniel B. Ullman. Cast: Joanne Dru, Peter Finch, Yvonne Furneaux, Patrick Holt, Michael Hordern.

49. KING'S RHAPSODY. An Everest Film, released by United Artists, 1955 (c). *Herbert Wilcox*. Sp: Pamela Bower and Christopher Hassall, and A.P. Horbert, b/o play by Ivor Novello. Cast: Anna Neagle, Patrice Wymore, Martita Hunt, Finlay Currie.

50. ISTANBUL. Universal, 1956 (c). *Joseph Pevney*. Sp: Seton I. Miller, Barbara Gray, and Richard Alan Simmons, b/o story by Seton I. Miller. Cast: Cornell Borchers, John Bentley, Torin Thatcher, Leif Erickson, Peggy Knudsen, Martin Benson, Nat King Cole, Werner Klemperer, Vladimir Sokoloff. A remake of *Singapore* (1947).

51. THE BIG BOODLE. United Artists, 1957. *Richard Wilson*. Sp: Jo Eisinger, b/o novel by Robert Sylvester. Cast: Pedro Armendariz, Rossana Rory, Gia Scala, Sandro Giglio, Jacques Aubuchon, Carlos Rivas, Charles Todd.

52. THE SUN ALSO RISES. 20th Century-Fox, 1957 (c). *Henry King*. Sp: Peter Viertel, b/o novel by Ernest Hemingway. Cast: Tyrone Power, Ava Gardner, Mel Ferrer, Eddie Albert, Gregory Ratoff, Juliette Greco, Marcel Dalio, Henry Daniell, Robert Evans.

53. TOO MUCH, TOO SOON. Warner Bros., 1958. *Art Napoleon*. Sp: Art and Jo Napoleon, b/o book by Diana Barrymore and Gerold Frank. Cast: Dorothy Malone, Efrem Zimbalist, Jr., Ray Danton, Neva Patterson, Murray Hamilton, Martin Milner, Kathleen Freeman, John Doucette.

54. THE ROOTS OF HEAVEN. 20th Century-Fox, 1958 (c). *John Huston*. Sp: Romain Gary and Patrick Leigh-Fermor, b/o novel by Romain Gary. Cast: Juliette Greco, Trevor Howard, Eddie Albert, Orson Welles, Paul Lukas, Herbert Lom, Gregoire Aslan, Andre Luguet, Friedrich Ledebur.

55. CUBAN REBEL GIRLS. Exploit Films, 1959. *Barry Mahon*. Sp: Errol Flynn. Cast: Beverly Aadland, John McKay, Jackie Jackler, Marie Edmund, Ben Ostrovsky, Regnier Sanchez.

INDEX

156

ABOUT THE AUTHOR

George Morris graduated from the University of Texas in 1967 with a Bachelor of Fine Arts degree. He has contributed film criticism frequently to *The Village Voice* and *The Real Paper*. He has also written articles for *Film Comment, The Solo Weekly News,* and *Changes.*

ABOUT THE EDITOR

Ted Sennett is the author of *Warner Brothers Presents,* a tribute to the great Warners films of the Thirties and Forties, and of *Lunatics and Lovers,* on the long-vanished but well-remembered "screwball" comedies of the past. He is also the editor of *The Movie Buff's* Book and has written about films for magazines and newspapers. He lives in New Jersey with his wife and three children.